this book belongs to

_____

Trisha's Kitchen

Trisha's Kitchen

EASY COMFORT FOOD for FRIENDS & FAMILY

TRISHA YEARWOOD

WITH BETH YEARWOOD BERNARD · FOREWORD BY GARTH BROOKS

HOUGHTON MIFFLIN HARCOURT
BOSTON NEW YORK 2021

For information about permission to reproduce selections
from this book, write to trade.permissions@hmhco.com or to Permissions,
Houghton Mifflin Harcourt Publishing Company,
3 Park Avenue, 19th Floor, New York, New York 10016.

hmhbooks.com

Library of Congress Cataloging-in-Publication Data is available.

ISBN 978-0-358-56737-0 (hbk)

ISBN 978-0-358-56733-2 (ebk)

ISBN 978-0-358-62128-7 (signed ed)

ISBN 978-0-358-67137-4 (signed ed bn)

ISBN 978-0-358-67456-6 (special ed)

Printed in the United States of America

4500829417

Connect with Trisha on social media:

FACEBOOK: www.facebook.com/TrishaYearwood
TWITTER: @TrishaYearwood
INSTAGRAM: @TrishaYearwood
YOUTUBE: www.youtube.com/TrishaYearwood
WEBSITE: www.trishayearwood.com

The kitchen has always been the heart of our home. We learned from the best. Our parents, Jack and Gwen Yearwood, showed us daily how to cook, how to laugh, how to bring that kitchen to life. Now that we're all grown up and have families of our own, we carry that tradition on. The kitchen is a place where you're always welcome. Come to help, or just to sit and talk while the meal gets prepared. This book is dedicated to all the home cooks— past, present, and future. You have our love and respect.

Love, Trisha and Beth

Contents

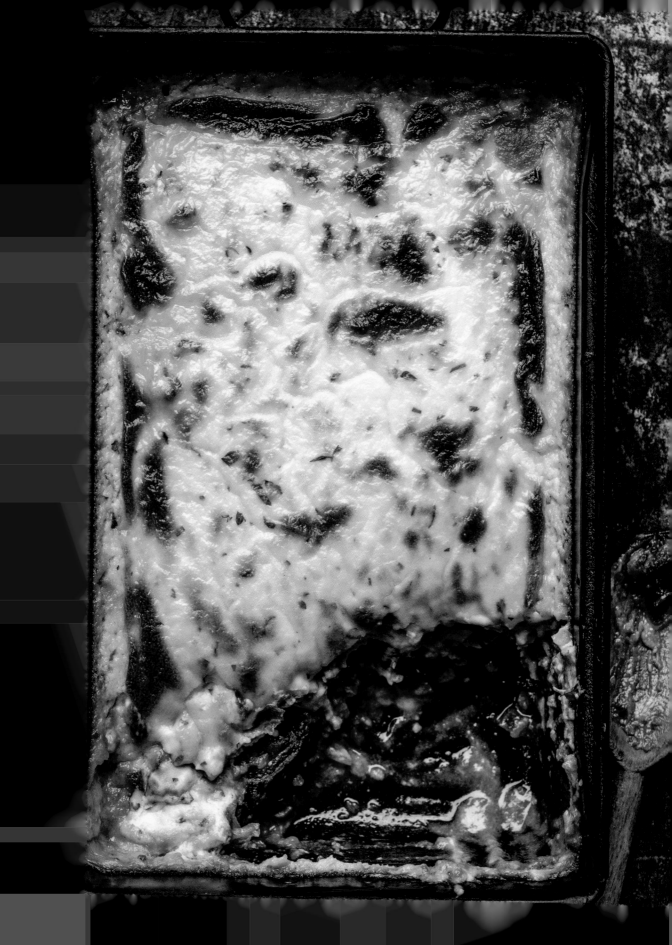

CHICKEN, TURKEY & FISH

VEGGIE NIGHT

BREADS

PRESERVES, PICKLES, SAUCES & SPREADS

SWEETS

FOREWORD

BY GARTH BROOKS

Miss Yearwood LOVES reading and cooking. She loves her dogs, music, and movies, too. One of our favorite movies is *The Shawshank Redemption*. From that movie comes one of the best lines ever: "A good thing never dies." In fact, a good thing only gets better with time, and THAT is Miss Yearwood. Her beauty, her voice, her cooking . . . just gets better with time. She calls cooking "therapy." It calms her, and coincidentally, her food calms all at her table. Ingredients, aromas, textures, presentation . . . she understands all the stages of a perfect meal. But even all of these combined do not make the perfect meal without love—the main ingredient in Trisha's kitchen.

I often describe dinner at our home very much like this: Trisha will prepare a meal like you would get at a five-star, very elegant restaurant, but you get to enjoy it in your favorite T-shirt and most comfortable pair of jeans AND it's okay that you're going to go back for seconds. Her birthday cakes, pies, and cobblers make all her friends wish to be another year older. Her cooking has become a tradition that our house and our future is built upon. Then, just when I think it can't get any better, I witness millions of people tuning into her show, tweeting and posting about how her recipes have brought their own families closer together. It is then I realize that what Trisha has done for our house, she has done for millions of households.

A good thing never dies . . . and the best example of that is love. Miss Yearwood is serving love to us as a generation, and that love will fill the plates of generations to come.

I'm so proud of you, Honey.

love, Garth

Introduction

IT WAS 1998, AND I FOUND MYSELF sitting in Maya Angelou's kitchen, watching her carefully bread fresh catfish in cornmeal. I was mesmerized by her fingers, as she gently coated each piece of fish with care, laughing and enjoying the time spent doing it. I had come by this coveted seat by some stroke of luck that I couldn't explain. I was on tour with Garth, and we were playing a show in Winston-Salem, North Carolina, near where Maya taught World Dramatic Poetry at Wake Forest University, when the call came that she'd like for me to come to lunch. Was this really happening to me? I couldn't believe it!

It's one of the most memorable days of my life. I knew I was at the School of Maya, and I didn't want to miss the lesson. I learned that day that communication and love are the most important things in life, and that they are served up well with a side of good food. That afternoon solidified my belief that food and relationships are so completely and utterly intertwined, and I live every day that way. Maya once said, "I'm just someone who likes cooking and for whom sharing food is a form of expression."

That connection is why I wrote my first cookbook, almost eight years later, and why I sit here still thinking about the people I love every time I cook a meal. I still had both of my parents in 1998, so I didn't know then the great loss their passing would bring. But I also didn't know the great comfort I would feel from the memories of them every time I made a meal from my childhood that they had perfected. I didn't know it that day, sitting in Miss Angelou's kitchen, but I think that deeper connection is part of what she was trying to teach me.

When that first cookbook, *Georgia Cooking in an Oklahoma Kitchen,* came out in 2006, I never would have dreamed that fifteen years later I'd be writing my fourth one. My original intention was to put all our family recipes into a book, with the help of my mom, Gwen, and my sister, Beth, and share our lives, stories, and food with all of you. We worked on that first book after my dad passed in 2005, and it was labor of love that brought us together and helped us pay homage to Jack Yearwood, husband, father, and great cook.

The TV show, *Trisha's Southern Kitchen,* came about in 2012, a few short months after Beth and I lost our mom to cancer. The show became a way for my sister and me to keep our mom and dad's memories alive through making those recipes, sharing them with a much bigger audience, and

"You don't have to cook fancy or complicated masterpieces—just good food from fresh ingredients." —JULIA CHILD

I hope you feel welcome. Pull up a
front-row seat. Everything is easy to make,
and everything is home-cooked.

telling our parents' stories. Every time we cooked a family recipe on the show, it felt like they were right there with us, guiding our hands and helping us tell those stories. It's been a wonderful tribute to our family to be able to share our lives in this way. I like to think my folks would be proud to see Mama's famous pimento cheese folded into creamy Southern grits, or my dad's easy biscuit recipe turned into an entire breakfast with country ham actually *in* the biscuit.

Beth and I have also created traditions of our own, like her classically Southern Shrimp and Grits or our Peach Preserves, which were born this year when Beth and her husband, John, relocated to Tennessee and purchased some land with a wonderful peach orchard on it. We made peach EVERYTHING, and you'll find those recipes here, along with all the stories—and every recipe *does* tell a story, whether it's my Grandma Yearwood's Hundred-Dollar Cupcakes from fifty years ago, or the Camo Cake that I made for my camo-loving compadre and nephew, Kyle.

What I can tell you is this: I love to cook now more than I ever have, because for me, cooking is about love. It's sharing a meal with family and friends and talking about our lives. It's working out thoughts in my head while I'm working on a homemade pastry crust—about what's going on with me, with my family, and what I need to conquer or accomplish. Sometimes the feel of the cold butter in my hands as I'm working it through the flour just makes me see things more clearly.

In fact, this book came to life during a time when were all grappling with the fear and uncertainty of a pandemic. Even in the worst of times, some good has come out of our being home. We've reconnected with friends and family like never before, we're eating together as a family more, we're reevaluating what's important in our lives, and we're cooking more. We're more in tune with our food, how it's grown, and how it gets to our table, and we're taking responsibility for providing that love and care to our families. That's the good news, even during the hard times. Everybody's canning and making sourdough bread, myself included!

One of the best compliments I receive about *Trisha's Southern Kitchen* is when someone who watches the show says, "I feel like I could be in the kitchen with you and it wouldn't be weird!" I smile all over when I hear that. That's exactly what I want. I want to make food that is simple and good. I want you to know you can do this! I'll hold your hand through anything that feels the least bit complicated, I promise.

One of my favorite quotes, attributed to Maya Angelou, is: "I've learned that people will forget what you said, people will forget what you did, but people will never forget how you made them feel." I hope you feel the love in these pages. I'm forever grateful for the time I get to spend in the kitchen with my family and friends, cooking, laughing, living. This book is as close as I can come to having you sitting next to me in the kitchen. I hope you feel welcome. Pull up a front-row seat. Everything is easy to make, and everything is home-cooked. Let's get started.

Love, Trisha

Useful Equipment & Substitutions

Everyday Items

THINGS YOU SHOULD ALWAYS STOCK
IN YOUR KITCHEN

- Mixing bowls of various sizes
- Cast-iron skillet, 8 to 10 inches
- Muffin tins/cupcake pans
- Large baking sheets
- Rimmed baking sheets (also called jelly-roll pans)
- Wire cooling racks
- Dutch oven or heavy-bottomed pan like cast-iron
- Electric hand mixer
- Food processor
- Grater
- Blender
- Mesh strainers
- Spatulas
- A good knife!
- Slotted spoons
- Colander
- Measuring spoons (several sets)
- Measuring cups (2 sets for dry ingredients and 2 measuring cups for liquids)

Special Equipment

ITEMS RECOMMENDED FOR THE RECIPES
IN THIS BOOK

- Round cookie cutters, various sizes
- Small (5-ounce) ramekins
- Instant Pot
- Slow cooker
- Immersion blender
- Digital kitchen scale
- Candy/deep-frying thermometer
- Meat thermometer

Wish List

THINGS YOU MAY NOT HAVE TO HAVE,
BUT YOU'LL WANT!

- High-powered blender, like a Vitamix
- Stand mixer, like a KitchenAid, with 2 bowls
- Charlotte pan (7-cup)
- Mini food processor
- Microplane grater, for zesting and finely grating
- Food mill
- Spider (large mesh spoon for deep-frying)

Substitutions

3 TEASPOONS = 1 tablespoon

1½ TEASPOONS = ½ tablespoon

2 TABLESPOONS = ⅛ cup

4 TABLESPOONS = ¼ cup

1 TABLESPOON FLOUR = 1½ teaspoons cornstarch

1 CUP SELF-RISING FLOUR = 1 cup sifted all-purpose flour + 1½ teaspoons baking powder + ⅛ teaspoon salt

1 CUP BUTTERMILK = 1 tablespoon lemon juice or white vinegar + enough whole milk to make 1 cup

1 CUP HALF-AND-HALF = 1½ tablespoons melted butter + enough whole milk to make 1 cup

1 TEASPOON VINEGAR = 2 teaspoons lemon juice

3 TABLESPOONS DRIED MINCED ONION = ½ cup raw onion

Breakfast

My favorite thing about breakfast is that you can enjoy it any time of day. The restaurants who advertise "Breakfast all day!"—those are my people. Whether you like savory dishes like quiches and casseroles or sweet ones like cinnamon rolls and sticky buns, I've got you covered!

BREAKFAST BURGERS

with Maple Hot Butter

Breakfast on the weekends has always been a big deal at my house. As a kid, I loved waking up late on Saturday mornings to the smell of my dad Jack's BIG breakfast cooking. Now that I'm all grown up, I relish a lazy weekend morning with my husband, and sometimes a daughter or a couple of friends stopping by to join us at the table for brunch. A late, lazy breakfast is where it's at in my family! I made this incredibly hearty burger for my family one weekend when I was testing recipes for a new season of *Trisha's Southern Kitchen*, and it became an instant classic. The maple hot butter is a bonus: easy to make and so worth it. Serve with Pimento Cheese and Bacon Grits (page 28).

SERVES 4

Burgers

½ pound bulk maple-flavored breakfast sausage

½ pound lean ground beef

3 tablespoons chopped fresh parsley

1 teaspoon kosher salt

½ teaspoon freshly ground black pepper

2 tablespoons butter

4 slices sharp cheddar cheese

French Toast Buns

½ cup heavy cream

½ cup whole milk

2 large eggs

4 potato buns

Maple Hot Butter

4 tablespoons (½ stick) butter

1 tablespoon pure maple syrup

1 tablespoon hot sauce (I like Tabasco)

1 avocado, sliced, for serving

1 **MAKE THE BURGERS:** In a large bowl, combine the sausage, beef, parsley, salt, and pepper. Use your hands to divide the meat into four 4-inch round patties.

2 Heat a large cast-iron skillet over medium heat until warm, about 1 minute, then add the butter. When the butter has melted, add the patties and pan-fry until they are evenly browned, 3 to 4 minutes per side. Use a spatula to flatten the patties as they cook. Lay a slice of cheese over each patty to melt. Transfer to a paper towel–lined plate and set aside.

3 **MAKE THE FRENCH TOAST BUNS:** In a medium bowl, whisk together the cream, milk, and eggs until thoroughly combined. Dip the potato buns briefly into the mixture to coat, about 10 seconds per half. Let the excess drip off, then put the buns into the skillet you just cooked the burgers in. Pan-fry over medium heat until golden brown and cooked through, about 2 minutes per side. Transfer to a plate.

4 **MAKE THE MAPLE BUTTER:** In a small saucepan, melt the butter over medium-low heat. Whisk in the maple syrup and hot sauce until fully combined. Remove from the heat.

5 To assemble the burgers, place the avocado slices on the bottom buns, then top with the patties, drizzle some maple butter over, then top with the bun tops and drizzle with a little more maple butter. Serve immediately.

HASH BROWN-CRUSTED ASPARAGUS SAUSAGE QUICHE

The first time I tried quiche was upstairs at the Davis-Kidd Booksellers restaurant here in Nashville. I was fresh out of Monticello, Georgia, and a student at Belmont College. Nineteen years old and I'd never tried quiche. I was an instant fan of the combination of breakfast staples all baked into a crispy crust. Quiche is such a versatile dish in that you can use whatever meats and veggies you like to make it suit your tastes. As long as you have eggs and cheese, the rest of the ingredients are up to you. The star of this show is the yummy hash brown crust. Be warned: You may never go back to regular quiche again! Serve this quiche alongside my Breakfast Burgers (page 20).

◆

SERVES 4 TO 6

3 cups frozen hash browns (about 10 ounces), thawed

4 tablespoons (½ stick) butter

Kosher salt and freshly ground black pepper

3 ounces bulk breakfast sausage

1 medium shallot, finely diced

5 medium stalks asparagus, cut in ½-inch pieces

⅓ cup grated sharp cheddar cheese

½ cup heavy cream

3 large eggs

1 tablespoon finely chopped fresh chives

Large pinch of cayenne pepper

1 Preheat the oven to 450°F.

2 Pat the hash browns dry and put them in a large bowl. In a medium skillet, melt 3 tablespoons of the butter over medium heat. Pour the butter over the hash browns, add a generous pinch each of salt and black pepper, and mix well. Press the hash browns over the bottom and up the sides of a 9-inch pie pan. Bake until golden brown, 20 to 25 minutes.

3 Meanwhile, in the same skillet, melt the remaining 1 tablespoon butter over medium-high heat. Add the sausage and sauté until just cooked through, 4 to 5 minutes. Add the shallot and asparagus and cook until the sausage is browned and the veggies are softened, about 6 minutes.

4 When the crust is ready, remove it from the oven and reduce the oven temperature to 375°F. Spoon the sausage and vegetables into the crust and sprinkle with the cheddar.

5 In a medium bowl, whisk together the cream, eggs, chives, cayenne, and ¼ teaspoon salt. Pour the mixture over the sausage mixture in the crust.

6 Bake the quiche until golden brown and just set in the center, 20 to 25 minutes. Let cool for at least 10 minutes before serving. Serve warm or at room temperature.

PECAN STICKY BUNS

with Bacon Caramel

Georgia is known for peanuts and peaches, but it also leads the nation in pecan production. We grew up with a huge pecan tree in the front yard, and Beth and I picked pecans up every fall for a few cents a pound. This sticky bun recipe takes those pecan swirls from the store that we ate growing up and turns them literally upside down! The bacon drippings in the caramel are the secret.

MAKES 12 BUNS

1 pound bacon

1½ cups packed light brown sugar

¼ cup pure maple syrup

¼ cup heavy cream

¼ teaspoon kosher salt

4 tablespoons (½ stick) butter

1 (17-ounce) box frozen puff pastry, thawed

1 tablespoon ground cinnamon

1½ cups pecans, chopped

1 Preheat the oven to 400°F. Place a 12-cup muffin tin on a baking sheet lined with parchment paper.

2 Using kitchen shears, cut the bacon into small pieces, dropping them into a medium stockpot. Cook over medium heat, stirring occasionally, until the bacon is almost crispy but not quite done, 6 to 8 minutes. Transfer the bacon to a paper towel–lined plate to drain.

3 Reduce the heat to medium-low and add 1 cup of the brown sugar to the bacon drippings in the pot. Cook, whisking frequently, until the sugar has dissolved, about 3 minutes. The mixture will look granular. Slowly stream in the maple syrup and whisk vigorously as the mixture begins to bubble. Once the syrup comes together, add the cream and salt. Remove from the heat and whisk until all the cream is incorporated. Set aside.

4 In a small saucepan, melt the butter over medium heat.

5 Unfold both sheets of puff pastry and arrange them so the fold lines run parallel to the counter edge. Generously brush the sheets with the melted butter. Combine the remaining ½ cup brown sugar with the cinnamon in a small bowl. Sprinkle the sugar mixture evenly over the buttered pastry sheets. Sprinkle ½ cup of the bacon and 1 cup of the pecans over the pastry and gently press the bacon and nuts into the sugar mixture with your palms. Roll up the pastry sheets away from you, forming 2 tight logs. Use a serrated knife to cut each log crosswise into 6 equal pieces.

6 Pour 1 tablespoon of the bacon-caramel sauce into each muffin cup. Sprinkle with 1 tablespoon each of the bacon and remaining pecans. Place a rolled bun cut-side down into each muffin cup and gently press down, maintaining their round shape.

7 Bake until the caramel bubbles and the buns are deeply golden brown, about 35 minutes. While they are still hot, work quickly to release the sides of the buns from the muffin cups with a small knife. Invert the muffin tin onto the baking sheet. Spoon any caramel that remains in the muffin tin over the buns. Serve immediately.

GARTH'S BREAKFAST LASAGNA

A lot of my new recipes come from conversations I have with Garth. He usually dreams up some idea and asks if I can figure out how to make it, and I'm always up for the challenge. We both love a late breakfast, and this lasagna ticks all the yummy boxes (and it's good for supper, too!) The cool thing about this concoction is that you can make it your own using your favorite breakfast meats, greens, and different kinds of veggies and cheeses.

SERVES 8

Nonstick cooking spray

1 (12-ounce) package center-cut bacon

2 tablespoons olive oil

1 pound bulk sage-flavored sausage

1 shallot, diced

1 (10-ounce) package frozen chopped spinach, thawed

1 (4-ounce) jar diced pimentos, drained

4 cups grated cheddar cheese

1½ cups grated Gruyère cheese

¼ cup all-purpose flour

2 cups whole milk

Kosher salt and freshly ground black pepper

9 oven-ready lasagna noodles

6 large eggs, whisked

1 Preheat the oven to 350°F. Spray a 9 x 13-inch baking pan with cooking spray.

2 Using kitchen shears, cut the bacon into small pieces, dropping them into a medium saucepot. Cook the bacon over medium heat until crispy, 5 to 7 minutes. Drain on a paper towel, and reserve ¼ cup of the drippings in the pot.

3 In a medium skillet, heat the oil over medium heat. Add the sausage and cook, breaking it up with a wooden spoon, until browned, 7 to 8 minutes. Remove the sausage with a slotted spoon and transfer to a medium bowl. Add the shallots to the skillet with the sausage drippings and cook for 1 to 2 minutes, until the shallots soften a bit. Stir in the spinach and pimentos and cook for 2 to 3 minutes, until heated through. Add the sausage and bacon to the spinach mixture and toss to combine. Set aside.

4 Mix the cheddar and Gruyère in a large bowl. Return the pot with the bacon drippings to medium heat. Whisk in the flour and cook, whisking, until slightly browned, about 2 minutes. Add the milk and continue whisking until slightly thickened, about 5 minutes. Remove the pan from the heat and add 3 cups of the grated cheeses. Stir until the cheese has melted, 1 to 2 minutes. Season with ½ teaspoon salt and ¼ teaspoon pepper.

5 Spread ¾ cup of the cheese sauce over the bottom of the prepared pan. Layer 3 noodles over the sauce. Top with one-third of the bacon-sausage mixture, one-quarter of the remaining grated cheeses, and one-third (about a heaping ½ cup) of the cheese sauce. Repeat the layers two more times, making sure all the top noodles are covered with the sauce.

6 Add 1 teaspoon salt and ½ teaspoon pepper to the whisked eggs and pour over the lasagna. Top with the remaining grated cheeses.

7 Bake for 40 to 45 minutes, until the cheese is golden brown and bubbling and the eggs are set. Remove from the oven and let rest for at least 15 minutes before serving.

I use sage-flavored sausage for Garth, but change things up by trying spicy or maple-flavored sausage.

PIMENTO CHEESE & BACON GRITS

Every now and then I'll come up with a recipe that combines all the things I love into one pan. This grits dish might be the trifecta, covering all the best flavors of the South. I add smoked Gouda to give it an even deeper, richer taste, but use whatever cheeses you love for these dressed-up grits. In *My Cousin Vinny,* shot in my hometown of Monticello, Georgia, Joe Pesci's character asks a witness if he uses instant grits. The witness replies, "No self-respecting Southerner uses instant grits!" I simply say, "To each his own!" Using the quick grits in this recipe gets them to the table faster!

SERVES 4 TO 6

4 slices thick-cut bacon, chopped into ¼-inch pieces

¼ cup sour cream

1 (4-ounce) jar diced pimentos, drained

4 ounces sharp cheddar cheese, grated

4 ounces smoked Gouda cheese, grated

1½ cups quick-cooking grits

2 teaspoons kosher salt

1 teaspoon freshly ground black pepper

2 tablespoons thinly sliced green onions

1 In a small skillet, cook the bacon over medium heat until crispy, about 10 minutes. Remove from the heat and let cool slightly, about 2 minutes, then transfer to a medium bowl. Stir in the sour cream and pimentos until combined and smooth. Add the cheddar and Gouda and stir until the mixture is thoroughly combined.

2 Meanwhile, in a large stockpot, bring 6 cups water to a boil. Add the grits, salt, and pepper and cook according to the package directions.

3 When the grits are cooked, pour the cheese mixture into the grits and stir until the cheese melts into the grits and is completely combined. Pour into a large serving bowl and top with the green onions before serving.

CHEESY BEEF & POTATO HASH

This hash takes me back to my early touring days, when, after a long night of traveling between shows, the tour bus would pull into some truck stop in the middle of nowhere to give our bus driver, Terry, a few minutes to refuel, grab some coffee, and gear up for the rest of the drive. Sometimes I would be up in the jump seat, keeping him company, and we'd watch the sun come up while we talked about life. On those early mornings, while everyone on the bus was still asleep, Terry and I would amble into the truck stop diner and have breakfast. I would almost always order some form of this recipe, and it was always served in a cast-iron skillet. We'd get back on the bus, I'd go back to sleep, tummy full, and Terry would get us where we needed to go. He drove my band and me for almost twenty years. Great food always goes hand in hand with great memories. This dish goes best with a big cup of coffee and a nap!

SERVES 4

2 medium russet potatoes

3 tablespoons olive oil

Kosher salt and freshly ground black pepper

1 small onion, diced

1 red bell pepper, diced

1 garlic clove, minced

½ pound extra-lean (90%) ground beef

½ teaspoon chili powder

1½ cups grated sharp cheddar cheese

1 Peel the potatoes and cut into small cubes (½ inch or less). Place them in a medium bowl with enough cool water to cover. Mix to rinse off excess starch, then drain and rinse in a colander. Pour out onto paper towels and pat dry.

2 In a 10-inch cast-iron skillet, heat the oil over medium-high heat. Add the potatoes and cook, stirring occasionally, until tender and golden brown on most sides, about 15 minutes. Season with ¼ teaspoon salt and black pepper to taste, then transfer to a plate with a slotted spoon.

3 Preheat the broiler to high.

4 Add the onion, bell pepper, and garlic to the same skillet and cook, stirring occasionally, until the onions start to brown, about 7 minutes. Add the beef and ½ teaspoon salt and cook, breaking up any clumps with a wooden spoon, until browned, 5 to 7 minutes. Stir in the chili powder until the beef is fully coated. Remove from the heat. Return the potatoes to the skillet and mix to combine.

5 Sprinkle the cheese over the hash. Broil until the cheese is melted and bubbling, about 1 minute. Serve warm.

GALAXY DOUGHNUTS

Doughnuts are one of those foods that work well for breakfast, a snack, or dessert. When I'm craving a doughnut, I love to make these beauties. If you aren't feeling the homemade doughnut step just yet, you can buy plain, unfrosted doughnuts at your local bakery. I love to make my own, especially when we have kids and grandkids over. They're easy to make and fun to decorate! My friends at Five Daughters Bakery here in Nashville, home of the 100-layer doughnut, even gave me a super-cool specialty cutter that makes perfectly round dough pieces with the holes punched for you, but two different sized round cookie cutters will do the trick here just as well! Dipping into the swirled glaze makes these doughnuts beautiful as well as sweet and tasty. Okay, I'll say it: These galaxy doughnuts are out of this world!

◆

MAKES 6 DOUGHNUTS

4 cups confectioners' sugar, plus more if needed

½ cup milk, plus more if needed

2 tablespoons coconut oil, liquid or melted from solid

1 tablespoon vanilla extract

Purple, black, pink, and blue gel food coloring

6 plain (unfrosted) doughnuts, store-bought, or try my Buttermilk Yeasted Doughnuts (page 35)

Food-grade edible silver glitter

1 In a large bowl, whisk together the confectioners' sugar, milk, coconut oil, and vanilla until smooth. Add more sugar if the mixture is too thin, or a little more milk if it's too thick; the icing should have a thick liquid consistency, not too drippy.

2 Add 2 drops of purple food coloring to the icing and mix to tint the base. Add 1 or 2 drops of each remaining color and swirl the surface of the icing several times with a skewer or toothpick, making sure not to overmix. (Coffee stirring sticks work well.)

3 Set a wire rack over a rimmed baking sheet. Dip one side of a doughnut into the icing, letting the excess drip off for a moment before turning it over and placing it icing-side up on the rack. Continue with the remaining doughnuts. As the food coloring drops becomes more muddled, every 2 or 3 doughnut dips, skim off the top layer of icing and add new color combinations.

4 Sprinkle the doughnuts with edible glitter and let the icing set completely before serving.

Recipe Continues

Buttermilk Yeasted Doughnuts

1 cup full-fat buttermilk

1 (¼-ounce) packet active dry yeast (2¼ teaspoons)

6 tablespoons (¾ stick) unsalted butter, melted

2 large eggs

1½ teaspoons vanilla extract

¼ cup sugar

1 teaspoon kosher salt

5 cups all-purpose flour, plus more for dusting

Vegetable oil, for frying

In a small saucepot, warm the buttermilk over medium heat to about 90°F, using a candy thermometer to check the temperature, then transfer it to the bowl of a stand mixer and sprinkle in the yeast. Stir slightly to submerge the yeast, then set aside to let the yeast activate and get foamy, about 5 minutes.

Attach the bowl to a stand mixer fitted with the dough hook. Add the melted butter, eggs, vanilla, sugar, and salt to the yeast mixture. Mix on medium speed to combine. Sift the flour, then add it slowly in two separate additions to the mixer bowl, mixing on low until just combined, about 2 minutes for each addition. Scrape the loose flour into the center as needed. Once all the flour is added, adjust the mixer speed to medium-high and knead the dough for 3 to 4 minutes, until the dough is smooth and comes away from the sides of the bowl cleanly.

Cover and set aside in a warm place until the dough has doubled in size, about 1 hour.

Dust your clean countertop and two baking sheets with a sprinkling of flour. Turn the dough out onto the counter, sprinkle a little flour on top, and roll the dough flat to a ½-inch thickness. Using a round cutter that is 3½ inches in diameter, cut out all the circles you can, then use a 1-inch round cutter to cut out the centers. Place the cut doughnuts and the holes on the floured baking sheets, 6 per sheet, spacing them about 2 inches apart. Gently knead the dough scraps together once or twice and cut out more doughnuts to get a total of 12. Cover each baking sheet with a clean dish towel and let rise in a warm place for 30 to 45 minutes.

While the doughnuts rise, fill a large Dutch oven with 3 inches of oil. Clip a deep-fry thermometer to its side and heat the oil over high heat to 360°F. Line a baking sheet with a few layers of paper towels and set it nearby.

Add 3 or 4 doughnuts to the hot oil at a time and fry for about 2 minutes per side, until golden brown. Use a wire scoop to lift the doughnuts out of the oil and transfer to the paper towel–lined baking sheet to drain and cool. After you're done frying all the doughnuts, fry the holes in one batch, about 2 minutes total, then transfer to the baking sheet to cool slightly.

When the doughnuts and doughnut holes are cool enough to touch, transfer them to a wire rack to cool completely before glazing.

Makes 12 doughnuts and 12 doughnut holes

If you don't have buttermilk, stir 1 tablespoon of lemon juice or vinegar into 1 cup of whole milk and let sit for 5 minutes before heating.

BLUEBERRY PANCAKE CAKE

I remember learning to make blueberry muffins as a young girl as one of my first baking lessons in the kitchen with my mom. I've turned that love of blueberries into a massive pancake "cake" that is baked in a cast-iron skillet. It's light and fluffy, like those awesome childhood muffins, but big enough to feed a crowd! Amp up plain corn syrup with cinnamon and vanilla, and you've got a fancy breakfast or decadent dessert.

SERVES 4 TO 6

Cake

2 cups all-purpose flour

½ cup packed light brown sugar

2 teaspoons baking powder

1 teaspoon kosher salt

2 cups blueberries

2 cups buttermilk

1 teaspoon vanilla extract

2 large eggs, lightly beaten

3 tablespoons vegetable oil

2 tablespoons unsalted butter

White Pancake Syrup

1 cup light corn syrup

1 tablespoon vanilla extract

Pinch of ground cinnamon

1 **MAKE THE CAKE:** Preheat the oven to 375°F. Place a 10-inch cast-iron skillet in the oven to preheat.

2 In a large bowl, whisk together the flour, brown sugar, baking powder, and salt. Add the blueberries and toss them gently in the flour mixture. This will help keep the blueberries from sinking to the bottom of the cake.

3 In a separate bowl, whisk together the buttermilk, vanilla, and eggs.

4 Remove the hot skillet from the oven and add the oil and butter to the skillet. Let the butter melt completely, then carefully pour the oil and butter into the buttermilk mixture and whisk until fully incorporated. Remember that the skillet is hot, so be sure to use a potholder or oven mitt when handling.

5 Add the wet mixture to the dry mixture and stir gently until combined and most of the lumps are gone. Pour the batter into the hot skillet. Bake until the cake is fluffy and golden brown and a toothpick inserted into the center comes out clean, 30 to 35 minutes.

6 **WHILE THE CAKE IS BAKING, MAKE THE PANCAKE SYRUP:** In a small saucepan, stir together the corn syrup, vanilla, and cinnamon. Cook over low heat until the syrup is warm and pourable.

7 Slice the warm cake into wedges and serve with the pancake syrup.

COFFEE COFFEE CAKE

Those of you who know me, know that I don't just love coffee . . . I *adore* it. I even have a dedicated Saturday morning Facebook Live show called *Coffee Talk,* where I sit (usually in my pj's) and drink—you guessed it—coffee and just talk about life with my friends. Coffee cake is a dessert that is so named because it's a wonderful dish served with coffee. I decided to up the ante and include coffee *in* the coffee cake! Have I said coffee enough? This cake goes great with a hot cup of coffee!

SERVES 8

Nonstick cooking spray

Crumb Topping

½ cup all-purpose flour

¼ cup packed light brown sugar

½ teaspoon ground cinnamon

½ teaspoon instant coffee

Pinch of kosher salt

4 tablespoons (½ stick) unsalted butter, melted

Cake

1¾ cups all-purpose flour

1¾ teaspoons baking powder

1¾ teaspoons baking soda

½ teaspoon ground cinnamon

½ teaspoon kosher salt

¼ teaspoon ground cardamom

½ cup strong brewed coffee, at room temperature

⅓ cup sour cream

1 cup (2 sticks) unsalted butter, at room temperature

1 cup granulated sugar

2 large eggs

1 teaspoon vanilla extract

1 Preheat the oven to 350°F. Spray a 9-inch square baking pan with cooking spray, line it with parchment paper, and spray again.

2 **MAKE THE CRUMB TOPPING:** In a medium bowl, mix the flour, brown sugar, cinnamon, instant coffee, and salt. Add the melted butter and mix until crumbs form that you can clump together in your hand. Set aside.

3 **MAKE THE CAKE:** In a medium bowl, whisk together the flour, baking powder, baking soda, cinnamon, salt, and cardamom. In a smaller bowl, whisk together the coffee and sour cream until smooth.

4 In the bowl of a stand mixer fitted with the paddle attachment, beat the butter and granulated sugar until light and fluffy. Add the eggs one at a time, mixing well after each addition. Add the vanilla and beat until the mixture is light and fluffy, about 5 minutes.

5 Starting and ending with the flour mixture, alternate adding the flour mixture and the coffee mixture to the stand mixer. Mix well, scraping the bowl after each addition.

6 Pour the batter into the prepared pan and top evenly with the crumb topping. Bake for 45 minutes, or until a toothpick inserted into the center comes out clean. Remove the cake from the oven and let cool in the pan for 20 minutes before cutting and serving.

BUTTERMILK CHEDDAR CORN CAKES

A couple of years ago, Garth and I had the pleasure of participating in Habitat for Humanity's Jimmy & Rosalynn Carter Work Project build in South Bend, Indiana. We've done over ten builds with the Carters, and in addition to being a small part of providing affordable housing all over the world with Habitat, we feel so lucky to have forged a friendship with these two most amazing volunteers with such hearts for service. One night, after a long day of swinging a hammer (yes, we actually build, but nobody works harder than the Carters!), the former President and Mrs. Carter invited us to dinner in the hotel restaurant. We had fresh corn cakes that night, and I've been thinking about them ever since. You can enjoy these corn cakes as a breakfast side or, if you wanna be like President Carter, have it for your main dish.

◆

SERVES 2 OR 3

½ cup all-purpose flour

½ cup yellow cornmeal

1 tablespoon sugar

1 tablespoon baking powder

1 teaspoon kosher salt

2 tablespoons unsalted butter, plus more for cooking corn cakes and serving

1 large egg

1 cup low-fat buttermilk

½ cup grated sharp cheddar cheese

⅓ cup canned corn kernels, drained and rinsed

1 tablespoon dried chives

Pure maple syrup, for serving (optional)

1   In a medium bowl, whisk together the flour, cornmeal, sugar, baking powder, and salt.

2   In a large nonstick skillet, melt the butter over medium heat, then set aside to cool.

3   In a large bowl, whisk together the egg and buttermilk. While whisking, pour in the melted butter and stir until combined. Stir in the dry ingredients until just combined. (Be sure not to overwork the batter.) Fold in the cheese, corn, and chives.

4   Place the skillet you used to melt the butter over medium heat and add just enough butter to coat the bottom. Ladle about ½ cup of the batter into the pan, spreading it gently to form a thick circle. Cook until bubbles appear on the surface, 1 to 2 minutes. Flip and cook until golden brown on the bottom, 1 to 2 minutes more. Transfer to a plate and repeat with the remaining batter, melting a small pat of butter in the skillet between batches (this will help the corn cakes rise). Serve immediately, with more butter and maple syrup, if desired.

KNIFE-AND-FORK BACON

I could devote an entire chapter, maybe even an entire book, to bacon. It's a food group in my family! My friend Michelle shared this recipe for slab bacon that only enhanced my bacon life, so I had to share it with you. If you can't find the bacon slab in the pork section of your local grocery store, ask your butcher to cut it for you. As you cook this slab low and slow in the oven, it caramelizes and becomes almost candied. It's a great appetizer for your table! I have so much more to say, so I wrote a little love letter to bacon (see page 42), along with other easy ways to prepare it. I heart bacon!

SERVES 4

1 tablespoon pure maple syrup

1 tablespoon light brown sugar

¼ teaspoon kosher salt

Pinch of cayenne pepper

1 (2 x 9-inch) piece slab bacon, about 2 inches thick

1 Preheat the oven to 300°F.

2 In a small bowl, whisk together the maple syrup, brown sugar, salt, cayenne, and ½ cup water.

3 Working across the slab of bacon on the fatty side, make ¼-inch-deep slices about every 2 inches. This will help the bacon from curling as it cooks. Place the bacon in a loaf pan and pour the maple sugar mixture over, flipping it a few times to coat, then set, fatty side down. Cover the pan tightly with aluminum foil and bake for 45 minutes. Remove from the oven. Flip the bacon fat-side up—it will be a little stiff and the fat will have started to become more translucent—and bake, uncovered, for 35 minutes more. At this stage the bacon will be tender and will have begun to caramelize. A good amount of fat will have rendered into the pan with the sauce.

4 Remove the bacon from the oven and place it on its side on a baking sheet. Pour off as much fat as possible from the liquid remaining in the loaf pan. Save the bacon fat for a future use and save the remaining liquid to add later.

5 Put the bacon on the baking sheet back in the oven for 8 minutes, then flip the slab to the other side and pour the pan juices over the slab. Bake one last time to caramelize the sauce on the outside, about 5 minutes.

6 Serve warm, with a knife and fork to share at the table.

TRISHA'S TIPS

If your bacon slab is too long, just trim it to fit your loaf pan. Pan-fry the leftover bits to use in salads or a topping for your baked potato!

If your bacon slab is thicker than 2 inches, add 10 minutes per ½ inch of thickness to the initial cooking time.

An Essay on Bacon

My entire life, when I needed cooked bacon, I put an average of five strips at a time into a large skillet and cooked them on my stovetop on medium to medium-high heat in batches until I got all the bacon cooked. This always ended up with bacon spatters all over my stovetop and hot bacon fat popping onto my person! And it just took forever. The cleanup was a mess. But here's the thing: I LOVE bacon. I ADORE it. Bacon ALWAYS, ALWAYS makes things taste better. So I've learned some new ways to cook bacon, and it's my joy to share them with you!

◆ 1 (12-OUNCE) PACKAGE BACON ◆

Baking Bacon

Preheat the oven to 400°F. Line two large rimmed baking sheets with aluminum foil.

Lay the bacon in a single layer on the prepared baking sheets. Make sure you don't overlap the slices. Bake to your desired level of crispiness, 20 to 25 minutes. I bake for 10 minutes, trade the pans to the different racks, then bake for another 10 or 15 minutes, depending on how crispy I want the bacon.

Drain on a paper towel-lined plate. Reserve the bacon drippings for later use. This bacon bakes flat, so it's great for sandwiches and burgers.

Crumbled Bacon

Using kitchen shears, cut the bacon into bite-sized pieces, dropping them into a large stockpot. Cook over medium-high heat, stirring occasionally, until the bacon is crispy, 5 to 7 minutes.

Drain on a paper towel-lined plate. This method is great for bacon crumbles used on salads and as toppings for nachos. Cutting the bacon ahead of cooking it keeps you from having to handle hot bacon after frying. The tall stockpot keeps the bacon fat from popping all over the stovetop.

A Note on Bacon Fat

My mama used to store bacon grease in a repurposed Maxwell House coffee can in the pantry. I used to do the same, until my friend Ree Drummond brought me some as a gift (yes, bacon drippings are a WONDERFUL gift!). She said she refrigerated hers, and I want to be like Ree, so now I do the same! The truth is, bacon fat can be stored either way, but stored at room temperature, it will go rancid faster than if it's stored in the refrigerator. If you do decide to store your bacon drippings at room temperature, keep them in a dark-colored container, tightly sealed, and strain out any bacon bits before storing so it lasts longer, just like my mama did! I store drippings at room temperature for up to 6 months, and in the refrigerator for up to a year.

SAUSAGE VEGGIE BREAKFAST CASSEROLE

I think every Southern family has a breakfast casserole recipe. Beth and I revamped that tried-and-true dish, giving it a lift with lots of good-for-you vegetables like mushrooms, leeks, spinach, and peppers. Personalize this casserole by making it with your favorite veggies. Garth and I like to substitute veggie sausage crumbles for the regular sausage sometimes, to make this a vegetarian breakfast! I serve this casserole in individual ramekins for fun, but you can bake it all in one 9 x 13-inch casserole pan for 40 to 45 minutes, if you prefer.

SERVES 4

Nonstick cooking spray

1 tablespoon extra-virgin olive oil

4 ounces bulk breakfast sausage (I like sage flavored)

4 ounces cremini mushrooms, sliced

1 small leek, cleaned and chopped

1 garlic clove, grated

½ red bell pepper, diced

¼ teaspoon hot paprika

Pinch of dry mustard powder

Kosher salt and freshly ground black pepper

8 ounces frozen chopped spinach, thawed, liquid squeezed out

4 large eggs

1 or 2 dashes hot sauce

3 ounces Gruyère cheese, grated

Special Equipment

4 (5-ounce) ramekins

1   Preheat the oven to 375°F. Spray four 5-ounce ramekins with cooking spray and set them on a rimmed baking sheet.

2   Heat a medium skillet over medium-high heat. Add the oil to heat, then add the sausage and cook, breaking up any big clumps with the back of a wooden spoon, until brown and crispy, 5 to 6 minutes. Transfer the sausage to a large bowl, leaving behind any rendered fat. Add the mushrooms and leeks to the skillet and cook until they are softened, 2 to 3 minutes. Add the garlic and bell pepper. Sprinkle in the paprika, mustard, ½ teaspoon salt, and ¼ teaspoon black pepper and cook for 5 to 8 minutes more.

3   Add the mushroom mixture to the bowl with the sausage. Stir together and add salt and black pepper to taste.

4   In a blender, combine the spinach, eggs, hot sauce, ¼ teaspoon salt, and ½ teaspoon black pepper. Blend until smooth. Stir the spinach mixture and the Gruyère into the sausage mixture a little at a time.

5   Pour the mixture into the prepared ramekins. Bake until the casseroles are entirely set, 30 to 35 minutes. Let the casseroles cool slightly before eating. Serve warm or at room temperature.

Individual casserole servings

GARTH'S PEACH KOLACHES

When my sister, Beth, bought some land with a peach orchard on it, we harvested peaches and made everything we could think of with the crop. We made preserves and crostatas, both featured in this book (see pages 213 and 250). Garth asked if I could make peach kolaches. My first question was, "What is a kolache?" I learned from him that it's a Czech-inspired pastry that he used to eat in Oklahoma. What? The history is that Czech immigrants settled in the Oklahoma Territory and brought with them their culture and cuisine, including the kolache. Garth grew up in Yukon, Oklahoma, and for over fifty years the town has been home to the Oklahoma Czech Festival, a huge annual outdoor event. The festival promotes and celebrates Yukon's Czech heritage with a carnival, parade, craft booths, music, dancing, games, and—you guessed it—kolaches. These pastries are so yummy. I was happy to re-create something from Garth's childhood that made him smile, and to find another tasty use for homegrown peaches!

MAKES 24 KOLACHES

2 cups milk

1 (¼-ounce) packet active dry yeast (2¼ teaspoons)

4 tablespoons (½ stick) butter

¼ cup solid shortening (I like Crisco sticks)

Nonstick cooking spray

2 large eggs

1¼ cups granulated sugar

2 teaspoons kosher salt

8 cups bread flour, plus more for dusting

2 large peaches, peeled, pitted, and chopped

1 cup peach preserves, store-bought or try Beth's Peach Preserves (page 213)

Sweet Sugar Drizzle

4 tablespoons (½ stick) butter, melted

1 teaspoon vanilla extract

2 cups confectioners' sugar

2 to 3 tablespoons heavy cream or milk

Pinch of kosher salt

1   In a medium saucepan, warm the milk over medium heat until it starts to steam (but not boil) and forms a skin on the surface. Take it off the heat and let cool slightly, 15 to 20 minutes; it should still be warm. Transfer ½ cup of the milk to a small bowl, add the yeast, and set aside until the yeast has dissolved and the mixture is foamy, about 5 minutes.

2   Meanwhile, in a medium microwave-safe bowl, microwave the butter and shortening together for 1 minute, stirring once halfway through, until melted and combined. Set aside to cool for 5 minutes.

3   Grease a large bowl with cooking spray and set aside.

4   In another large bowl, mix together the eggs, granulated sugar, salt, and butter-shortening mixture. Add the reserved milk and the yeast mixture and stir to combine. Slowly add the bread flour, 1 cup at a time, mixing with a fork or your hands until the flour is incorporated. Turn the dough out onto a board or kitchen counter lightly dusted with bread flour and form into a ball; it will be slightly sticky to the touch. Don't overwork this dough, or it will be tough. Put the dough ball in the greased bowl. Cover with plastic wrap and let the dough rise until it doubles in size, about an hour.

Kolaches, hot out of the oven

5 Punch down the dough to deflate, cover again with the plastic wrap, and refrigerate for at least 4 hours or up to overnight.

6 In a medium bowl, mix the peaches with the preserves and set aside.

7 Spray two large (13 x 18-inch) baking sheets with cooking spray. Remove the dough from the fridge, shape it into balls 3 inches in diameter, and place them on the prepared baking sheets, about 3½ inches apart. You should be able to get 12 on each baking sheet. Using the bottom of a small jar or the back of a spoon, press down in the middle of each ball to make a space for the filling and dollop 2 tablespoons of the filling in each. Cover the kolaches with plastic wrap and let rise until doubled in size, about 1 hour.

8 Preheat the oven to 375°F.

9 Bake the kolaches for 25 to 30 minutes, until light and golden brown.

10 MEANWHILE, MAKE THE GLAZE: In a medium bowl, whisk together the melted butter, vanilla, and sugar. Add the cream 1 tablespoon at a time until you get a thick but spreadable consistency. Whisk in the salt.

11 Using a pastry brush, brush the sides of the kolaches generously with the glaze. Serve warm.

EGGS IN PURGATORY

One of my friend Joe's favorite lines is from a movie called *Return to Me,* starring Minnie Driver. One night, Minnie's character's granddad, played by Carroll O'Connor, is playing cards with his buddies and his character says, "You're gonna be a long while in purgatory, you are!" and Robert Loggia's character says, "Really. Well, I'll be with friends!" It's fitting that the first time I made this dish for Garth, we had our friends Joe and Kim visiting from Oklahoma. It's the perfect late-morning hearty breakfast for your family or your visiting besties. The focaccia croutons take this dish to Heaven! For a special finish, add some easy spicy yogurt sauce.

SERVES 6

6 plum tomatoes
(2 pounds), quartered

1 large red bell pepper,
quartered

½ cup olive oil

2 tablespoons balsamic
vinegar

Kosher salt and freshly
ground black pepper

1 (1-pound) loaf focaccia,
store-bought or try my
Herbed Focaccia Bread
(page 189)

½ medium onion, finely
chopped

2 garlic cloves, minced

¼ teaspoon red pepper
flakes

6 large eggs, at room
temperature

Spicy Yogurt Sauce
(recipe follows), for
serving

Fresh oregano leaves, for
garnish, optional

1   Preheat the oven to 400°F, with a rack in the center. Line a rimmed baking sheet with parchment paper.

2   In a medium bowl, combine the tomatoes, bell pepper, ¼ cup of the olive oil, the vinegar, and a big pinch each of salt and black pepper. Toss gently to combine. Spread on the prepared baking sheet with the tomatoes skin-side down. Roast for 30 minutes, or until the tops of the tomatoes have caramelized. Remove from the oven (keep the oven on) and, using tongs, transfer the tomatoes, peppers, and pan juices to a food processor or blender. Carefully pulse into a chunky sauce.

3   Tear the focaccia into chunks 2 to 3 inches in size and toss with 2 tablespoons of the olive oil. Spread over a baking sheet. After the vegetables are out of the oven, toast the focaccia pieces for 6 to 8 minutes, then remove from the oven and set aside.

4   Heat a large nonstick skillet over medium heat. Add the remaining 2 tablespoons olive oil and the onion, garlic, and red pepper flakes. Cook, stirring occasionally, until softened, about 4 minutes. Add the tomato-pepper sauce and ½ cup water, cover the pan with the lid ajar, and cook, stirring occasionally, until slightly thickened, about 10 minutes.

5   Crack an egg into a small bowl and then make a little indentation in the tomato sauce in the pan. Gently pour the egg into the indentation. Repeat with the remaining eggs. Cover the pan and cook, gently rotating the pan occasionally to make sure the eggs cook evenly, until the egg whites are set but the yolks are still runny, 5 to 7 minutes.

6   Serve in shallow bowls, topped with a few focaccia croutons, drizzled with yogurt sauce and sprinkled with fresh oregano if you like.

Recipe Continues

Spicy Yogurt Sauce

½ cup plain Greek yogurt

2 tablespoons olive oil

Zest and juice of 1 lemon

1 teaspoon finely chopped fresh oregano

1 teaspoon finely chopped fresh parsley

Pinch of red pepper flakes

Pinch of cayenne pepper (optional)

Kosher salt and freshly ground black pepper

In a medium bowl, whisk together the yogurt, oil, lemon zest, lemon juice, oregano, parsley, red pepper flakes, cayenne pepper, and 2 tablespoons water. Season with a heavy pinch each of salt and black pepper.

Makes about ¾ cup

Rinse the bowl you'll be cracking the eggs into with some room-temperature water. It will help the egg slide out of the bowl easily.

When blending the tomatoes and peppers, if you are using a blender, leave the top slightly "burped" and covered loosely with a dish towel so you can release pressure from the hot mixture without splashing yourself. If you're using a food processor, cover the open hole at the top with a dish towel before processing to prevent splashing. You can also use an immersion blender for this step.

OVERNIGHT CINNAMON ROLLS

This recipe comes from Beth's friend Leeann, who was once the breakfast chef at a guest ranch in Wyoming. During her time at the ranch, Leeann made hundreds of these cinnamon rolls. They're great for holidays and brunches, as most of the work is done the night before. Leeann is now an ordained Episcopal priest, so I guess we could call them holy rolls!

MAKES 12 ROLLS

Cinnamon Rolls

1½ cups warm water (105° to 110°F)

¾ teaspoon active dry yeast

½ cup granulated sugar, plus a pinch

½ cup (1 stick) unsalted butter

2 teaspoons kosher salt

1 large egg, at room temperature

6 to 6½ cups all-purpose flour, plus more for dusting

2 tablespoons canola oil

¼ cup packed light brown sugar

1 tablespoon ground cinnamon

Glaze

1¼ cups confectioners' sugar

½ teaspoon vanilla extract

Pinch of kosher salt

3 tablespoons milk

2 tablespoons butter, for serving

1 **MAKE THE CINNAMON ROLLS**: In the bowl of a stand mixer, stir together the warm water, yeast, and a pinch of sugar then set aside until it foams, 4 to 6 minutes.

2 Meanwhile, in a small saucepan, melt 4 table-spoons (½ stick) of the butter. Remove from the heat and let cool slightly.

3 Add the melted butter, granulated sugar, salt, and egg to the bowl with the yeast mixture. Using the whisk attachment, mix on medium speed to combine, about 2 minutes. Switch out the whisk for the dough hook and, with the mixer on low, stir in 1 cup of the flour at a time. The dough will be sticky and begin pulling away from the bowl in about 5 minutes.

4 Grease a large bowl with the oil. Fold the dough over itself 2 or 3 times in the mixer bowl, forming it into a ball, then transfer it to the greased bowl, rolling the dough over to coat with the oil. Cover with a damp towel and let the dough rise for 4 hours, punching it down every hour.

5 In the same small saucepan, melt the remaining 4 tablespoons butter. In a small bowl, combine the brown sugar and cinnamon.

6 Flip the dough out onto a floured surface and lightly flour the top of the dough. Using a rolling pin, roll out the dough into a rectangle, about 12 x 18 inches and ¼ inch thick. Brush the rectangle with 3 tablespoons of the melted butter, leaving the one long edge closest to you unbuttered. Sprinkle liberally with the cinnamon sugar.

7 Working from the unbuttered side, tightly roll the dough away from you and then lightly push the ends in to form an even log. Using thin string or unflavored dental floss, cut the log crosswise into 12 even rolls by placing the string under the log and crisscrossing it over the top to cut through. You can use a knife to cut the rolls, but they will retain their round shape better if you use floss.

Recipe Continues

8 Use the remaining melted butter to heavily grease a 9 x 13-inch glass baking dish. Place the rolls cut-side up in the dish, evenly spaced apart. The rolls will fill in any open space as they rise. Cover tightly with parchment paper, then a damp towel, and let rise on your counter for 6 hours or in the fridge overnight, until they have expanded to fill the pan.

9 When you're ready to bake the rolls, preheat the oven to 350°F.

10 Uncover the rolls and bake until tops are golden brown, 25 to 30 minutes.

11 **MEANWHILE, MAKE THE GLAZE:** In a small bowl, stir together the confectioners' sugar, vanilla, and salt, then slowly stir in the milk, 1 tablespoon at a time, to make a thick glaze that will stick to the rolls but still drip into all the nooks and crannies.

12 While the rolls are still hot from the oven, melt the 2 tablespoons butter and brush it over the tops of the rolls. Drizzle the glaze over the rolls and serve warm.

Snacks & Appetizers

Garth and I moved back to Nashville in 2014, after our girls were grown and off to college. Our home is always open, and friends and family often drop by unannounced. I love to keep snacks on hand, so you'll usually find some kind of dip or finger food on the ready for just such an occasion. You'll find all of my hearty go-to recipes in this section. My love of Nashville shows up in some hot chicken appetizers, and my Georgia roots make an appearance in dishes like spicy pimento cheese and a fun twist on collard greens!

NASHVILLE HOT CHICKEN MEATBALL SLIDERS

When I first moved to Nashville, the only place to get hot chicken was Prince's Hot Chicken on Ewing Drive. These days, hot chicken is all the rage in Nashville, and you can find it in a lot of restaurants. I love it all, but Prince's is still the gold standard for me. These sliders are my nod to Ms. André Prince Jeffries, who still serves up the best hot chicken I've ever tasted!

MAKES 12 SLIDERS

Meatballs

1 pound ground chicken

1 tablespoon Louisiana hot sauce

1 tablespoon light brown sugar

1 teaspoon smoked paprika

½ teaspoon kosher salt

¼ teaspoon freshly ground black pepper

¼ teaspoon cayenne pepper

2 garlic cloves, minced

2 ounces blue cheese, cut into 12 (¼-inch) cubes

2 tablespoons butter

1 tablespoon vegetable oil

Sauce

½ cup (1 stick) butter

½ cup Louisiana hot sauce

2 tablespoons honey

2 tablespoons light brown sugar

1½ teaspoons garlic powder

1 teaspoon kosher salt

¼ teaspoon freshly ground black pepper

2 tablespoons chopped fresh parsley

Sliders

Pickle chips (I like bread-and-butter pickles)

12 slider buns

1 **MAKE THE MEATBALLS:** Preheat the oven to 375°F.

2 In a large bowl, combine the ground chicken, hot sauce, brown sugar, paprika, salt, black pepper, cayenne, and garlic and gently mix with your hands until combined.

3 Divide the meat mixture into 12 portions, then form them into meatballs using wet hands. (Meat sticks to dry hands.) Push a piece of cheese into each meatball and pinch the meat mixture around it to enclose the cheese.

4 In a large ovenproof sauté pan, heat the butter and vegetable oil over medium heat until combined and shimmering, about 2 minutes. Add the meatballs and brown on all sides, 5 to 8 minutes. Transfer the pan to the oven and bake for 10 minutes to finish cooking the meatballs.

5 **MEANWHILE, MAKE THE SAUCE:** In a small saucepot, combine the butter, hot sauce, honey, and brown sugar. Bring to a boil over high heat, stirring continuously, then reduce the heat to medium and cook until the mixture comes together, 2 to 3 minutes. Remove from the heat, add the garlic powder, salt, and pepper and stir until smooth.

6 Remove the meatballs from the oven and pour the sauce over them. Toss to coat. Sprinkle with the parsley. Add a pickle chip to each bun, then set a meatball on top. Skewer with a toothpick. Serve warm.

RICOTTA TARTLETS

with Cherry Tomatoes

I gravitate toward simple dishes that look elegant and taste great. I learned from my mom, Gwen—the ultimate home cook, in my opinion—that simple is best, but that doesn't have to mean simple in taste. These tarts served warm are a wonderful appetizer for a party, and also make a great snack the next day. Prepackaged refrigerated pie crusts keep this snack super easy to put together.

MAKES 10 SMALL TARTS

---

1 (14.1-ounce) package refrigerated pie crusts (2 rounds)

½ cup whole-milk ricotta cheese

2 tablespoons grated Parmesan cheese

½ teaspoon Italian seasoning

1 large egg yolk

Kosher salt and freshly ground black pepper

1½ cups cherry tomatoes, halved

½ small shallot, very thinly sliced

1 tablespoon fresh thyme leaves

4 teaspoons olive oil

Special Equipment
4½-inch round cookie cutter (see Tips)

1   Preheat the oven to 400°F. Line two baking sheets with parchment paper.

2   Remove the pie crusts from the refrigerator to soften a little while you make the filling, but not to room temperature.

3   In a medium bowl, stir together the ricotta, Parmesan, Italian seasoning, egg yolk, a large pinch of salt, and a few grinds of pepper.

4   Unroll the pie crusts and cut out 10 rounds with a 4½-inch round cookie cutter, rerolling as needed. Lay the rounds out on a work surface and dollop a level tablespoon of the ricotta mixture in the center of each. Spread the ricotta over the round, leaving a ¼-inch border. Arrange the tomato halves in the center of the ricotta (4 or 5 halves per tart), leaving a ¼-inch border of ricotta. Fold and crimp the edges of the crust just over the exposed ricotta, but leaving the tomatoes uncovered. Sprinkle the shallot and thyme on top of the tomatoes, drizzle with the oil, and sprinkle with a little salt and pepper.

5   Transfer the tarts to the prepared baking sheets and bake until the crust is golden brown and the tomatoes are softened and lightly browned in spots, 15 to 20 minutes. Serve warm or at room temperature.

If you have loose or runny ricotta, line a fine-mesh strainer with cheesecloth, set it over a bowl, and strain the ricotta for 1 to 2 hours in the fridge before using.

If you don't have a 4½-inch cookie cutter, you can use the lid of a jar around the same size.

SWEET & SPICY MEATBALLS

My friend Lisa *has* to have something hot and spicy at every meal, so whenever we have a get-together, I make sure there is something she'll love. These sweet-and-spicy meatballs are the ticket! The sweetness of the pomegranate glaze balances out the heat of the jalapeños and the pepper jelly. I love the touch of adding pomegranate seeds as a garnish. It gives everybody a little hint of what's in the sauce. These meatballs are a big hit at holiday parties at my house!

MAKES 30 MEATBALLS

Nonstick cooking spray

½ pound ground beef

½ pound ground pork

1 (4-ounce) can diced jalapeños, drained

½ cup panko bread crumbs

1 teaspoon granulated garlic

1 large egg

1 small onion, finely chopped

1 (10-ounce) jar hot pepper jelly

½ teaspoon kosher salt

¼ teaspoon freshly ground black pepper

½ cup Bloody Mary mix

¼ cup pomegranate juice

2 tablespoons light brown sugar

¼ cup pomegranate seeds

1 Preheat the oven to 400°F. Place a wire rack on a rimmed baking sheet and lightly spray with cooking spray.

2 In a large bowl, combine the ground beef, ground pork, jalapeños, panko, garlic, egg, onion, 1 tablespoon of the pepper jelly, the salt, and the black pepper and gently fold the mixture together using a spatula or your hands.

3 Using a small scoop (I use a small ice cream scoop), roll a tablespoon of the meat mixture into a ball. Place it on the prepared rack and repeat until all the meat has been shaped into balls. Roast the meatballs until slightly browned, about 25 minutes.

4 Meanwhile, in a small saucepot, combine the Bloody Mary mix, pomegranate juice, brown sugar, and remaining pepper jelly (about ¾ cup). Bring to a boil over medium heat, stirring occasionally, and cook until the jelly has dissolved and the mixture has reduced slightly, about 5 minutes. Turn off the heat and pour the glaze into a large bowl to cool. The glaze will thicken as it cools.

5 Transfer the hot meatballs to the bowl with the glaze and gently toss until evenly coated. Transfer to a serving platter and garnish with the pomegranate seeds.

Try my Spicy Red Pepper Jelly (page 205) in the meatballs and the glaze.

COUNTRY HAM BISCUITS & JALAPEÑO PIMENTO CHEESE

with Fried Green Tomatoes

There are so many things to love about these biscuits! Country ham *inside* the biscuit, classic Southern pimento cheese with a kick, all topped off with a fried green tomato. People always ask if green tomatoes are unripe red tomatoes or their own variety. Both are correct! Ripe green tomatoes are usually heirlooms, and they will be softer to the touch, like a ripe red tomato. Unripe red tomatoes (aka green tomatoes) are the kind you want to use here, because they are firm and will hold up better for frying. These gems were made famous at the Whistle Stop Cafe in Juliette, Georgia, the setting for the 1991 film *Fried Green Tomatoes.* These biscuits are the essence of everything I love about Southern food.

MAKES 16 BISCUITS

Jalapeño Pimento Cheese

2 (7-ounce) bricks sharp white cheddar cheese, finely grated

1 (4-ounce) jar diced pimentos, drained

2 tablespoons diced pickled jalapeños, drained

½ cup mayonnaise

¼ cup chopped green onions

Kosher salt and freshly ground black pepper

Country Ham Biscuits

2 cups all-purpose flour, plus more for dusting

1 tablespoon baking powder

¼ teaspoon kosher salt

4 tablespoons (½ stick) unsalted butter, cubed and chilled, plus 1 tablespoon

¾ cup buttermilk, well shaken

¼ cup finely chopped country ham

16 Fried Green Tomatoes (recipe follows), for serving

1 Preheat the oven to 450°F. Place a 10-inch cast-iron skillet in the oven to preheat.

2 **MAKE THE PIMENTO CHEESE:** In a large bowl, stir together the cheese, pimentos, jalapeños, mayonnaise, and green onions. Season with salt and pepper. Set aside, or if making ahead, place in the fridge until ready to use.

3 **MAKE THE BISCUITS:** In a large bowl, mix the flour, baking powder, and salt. Using a pastry blender or two table knives, cut 4 tablespoons (½ stick) of the cold butter into the flour until it resembles a coarse meal. Using a fork, stir in the buttermilk to make a soft dough, stirring until the dough comes together and leaves the sides of the bowl. Continue stirring with the fork until all the flour is worked into the dough, then stir in the ham. Turn the dough out onto a lightly floured board and knead 3 or 4 times, until smooth and manageable.

4 With your hands or a floured rolling pin, flatten the dough to a thickness of ½ inch. Cut the dough with a floured 2-inch biscuit cutter. You may need to gather and reroll the dough scraps to cut the last couple of biscuits.

5 Remove the skillet from the oven and melt the remaining 1 tablespoon butter in the skillet. Place the biscuits in the skillet, 1 inch apart for crisp biscuits or almost touching for softer biscuits. Bake until lightly browned, 10 to 12 minutes.

6 To serve, split the biscuits, spread generously with the pimento cheese, and top with a fried green tomato.

Recipe Continues

Fried Green Tomatoes

2 quarts vegetable oil, for frying

1½ cups all-purpose flour

1 teaspoon kosher salt, plus more as needed

½ teaspoon freshly ground black pepper

4 large eggs

½ cup buttermilk

2 cups yellow cornmeal

1 cup panko bread crumbs

4 green tomatoes (about 1 pound total), sliced ¼ inch thick

Pour the oil into a Dutch oven or other heavy-bottomed pot. Clip a deep-fry thermometer to its side and heat the oil over medium heat to 350°F. Line a rimmed baking sheet with paper towels and top with a wire rack; set this nearby.

Set up three shallow dishes to make a breading station. In the first dish, stir together the flour, salt, and pepper. In the second dish, whisk the eggs and buttermilk together. In the third dish, stir together the cornmeal and panko.

Using one hand, dredge both sides of the tomato slices in the seasoned flour, shaking each piece to remove any excess. Next, using the other hand, dip the tomato slices in the egg mixture, allowing any excess to drip off before moving on to the third dish. Using your first hand, coat the tomato slices in the panko mixture evenly on both sides. (This method allows you to keep your dry hand dry and your wet hand wet.)

Working in batches, carefully place the breaded tomatoes into the hot oil and fry until golden brown and crispy, about 30 seconds per side. Transfer the fried tomatoes to the rack and sprinkle each slice generously with more salt.

Makes 16 slices

TRISHA's TIPS

When whisking together eggs and any other liquid, break up the egg yolks first. It makes the whisking much easier. Otherwise, you end up chasing whole yolks around your bowl!

If you'd rather bake the tomatoes than fry them, after breading, drizzle them on both sides with a little olive oil. Place them on a baking sheet and bake at 350°F for 7 to 8 minutes on one side, then flip and bake for 7 to 8 minutes more, until brown and crispy.

My mom, Gwen, and her pals Lin and Gail at the Whistle Stop Cafe, 1990s

CHIPOTLE CHICKEN TACO–STUFFED POTATO SKINS

When I was a kid, I looked forward to taco night. It was a rare treat for us—Mama would buy the shells and make the meat filling and all the toppings, and let us put together our own tacos. Another special-occasion dish was her twice-baked potatoes, which I REALLY loved. It was like dressing your own baked potato without having to do any of the work! These potato skins combine everything great about the stuffed potatoes of my childhood paired with the grown-up flavors of chipotles in adobo sauce. Chipotle chiles are dried, smoked jalapeños. They add an intense, smoky heat, while the tangy adobo sauce adds some sweetness. If you're worried about too much spice, use less fresh jalapeño in these stuffed treats. Potato skins are a must at Yearwood-Brooks get-togethers. Get ready for the "WOW!" when you serve these dressed-up skins at your next party.

SERVES 6 TO 8

8 small russet potatoes (about 4 pounds total), washed and dried

2 pounds boneless, skinless chicken breasts (4 or 5 breasts)

Kosher salt and freshly ground black pepper

5 tablespoons olive oil

1 large onion, finely chopped

1 to 2 small jalapeños (depending on how spicy you want it), seeded and finely chopped

½ cup jarred mild or medium salsa, smooth restaurant style

½ teaspoon ground cumin

2 canned chipotle chiles in adobo, seeded and finely chopped, plus 2 teaspoons adobo sauce from the can

½ cup heavy cream

2 cups grated cheddar cheese

3 green onions, finely chopped, for serving

3 tomatoes, chopped, for serving

2 avocados, chopped, for serving

Sour cream, for serving

Chopped fresh cilantro, for garnish

1 Preheat the oven to 400°F, with racks in the upper and lower thirds.

2 Pierce the potatoes two or three times with the tip of a sharp knife and arrange them evenly spaced on a baking sheet. Roast on the lower rack in the oven until the potatoes are easily pierced with the tip of a sharp knife, about 1 hour.

3 Meanwhile, season the chicken breasts all over with 1 teaspoon salt and 1 teaspoon pepper, then coat with 3 tablespoons of the oil. Place on a baking sheet and roast on the upper rack (above the potatoes) for 20 to 25 minutes, until just cooked through. The chicken is done when its internal temperature is 165°F. Let the chicken cool slightly, then finely chop each breast while the potatoes finish cooking.

4 When the potatoes are done, let them cool slightly, then halve them lengthwise. Using a small spoon, gently scoop the potato flesh into a bowl, leaving about ½ inch on the skins. Set the skins aside. Reserve the potato flesh for another use.

Recipe Continues

Charred
Red Salsa
65

Charred
Green Salsa
65

5   In a large skillet, heat the remaining 2 tablespoons oil over medium heat. Add the onion and jalapeños and cook, stirring occasionally, until soft, 7 to 8 minutes.

6   Stir in the chicken, salsa, cumin, chipotles and adobo sauce, and a pinch each of salt and pepper to combine. Cook 4 to 5 minutes, until everything is combined and heated through.

7   Reduce the heat to low, add the cream, and cook, stirring, until incorporated and heated through, about 1 minute.

8   Preheat the broiler to high. Line a baking sheet with parchment paper.

9   Spoon the chicken mixture into the hollowed-out potato skins. Put the potato skins on the prepared baking sheet. Sprinkle with the cheddar and broil on the upper rack until the cheese is melted, about 3 minutes. Transfer the skins to a serving platter and top with the green onions, tomatoes, avocados, sour cream, and cilantro.

TRISHA'S TIPS

Leftover potato flesh is great for potato soup, potato pancakes, or any other dish calling for potatoes. Don't throw it away! Store it in an airtight container in the freezer for up to 3 months.

Baking these russets unwrapped (instead of wrapped in foil like you would for baked potatoes) makes for a stronger potato skin, which helps keep them from breaking apart when you scoop out the insides.

CHARRED SALSA, TWO WAYS

I first ate at Uncle Julio's Mexican restaurant when I was traveling through Texas on tour in the '90s. I had a frozen margarita and sangria swirl that changed my life. Really! There are locations all over the Midwest and East Coast. I love their fresh salsas served with bottomless tortilla chips. The secret to the incredible taste of these salsas is literally charring the vegetables, letting them blacken on your grill. That's what gives both the green and red salsas their unique depth of flavor. It's also super easy to turn one salsa into another, so you can give your guests two choices with very little work (see photos, page 63). Thanks for the inspiration, Uncle Julio's!

SERVES 6

3 tomatillos (about 8 ounces total), husked and rinsed (see Tips)

1 Vidalia onion, cut into thick rounds

1 jalapeño

1 poblano pepper

4 tablespoons vegetable oil

Kosher salt

1 garlic clove, peeled

Juice of 1 lime (about 2 tablespoons)

¼ cup olive oil

½ cup packed fresh cilantro leaves

1 tablespoon sugar

1 (14.5-ounce) can diced fire-roasted tomatoes

Multicolored tortilla chips, for serving

1 Heat a grill pan over medium-high heat for 5 minutes. Meanwhile, put the tomatillos, onion, jalapeño, and poblano in a large bowl. Drizzle with 3 tablespoons of the vegetable oil, sprinkle generously with salt, and toss to evenly coat the vegetables. Brush the hot grill with the remaining 1 tablespoon vegetable oil.

2 Grill the vegetables, turning occasionally, until they are charred and softened, 12 to 15 minutes. Transfer the tomatillos and onion to a food processor. Transfer the peppers to a cutting board to cool briefly. Trim the stems off the peppers, then add the peppers to the food processor.

3 Add the garlic and lime juice to the food processor and pulse until the vegetables form a thick paste, about 2 minutes. With the processor on, slowly drizzle in the olive oil. Turn off the machine, add the cilantro, sugar, and 1 teaspoon salt, and pulse until smooth. Transfer 1 cup of the green salsa to a small serving bowl and set aside.

4 To the salsa remaining in the food processor, add the tomatoes. Pulse for 1 minute, until a smooth red salsa is formed, then transfer to a small serving bowl. Serve both salsas with tortilla chips.

TRISHA'S TIPS

Tomatillos are a husk tomato native to Mexico. They are more acidic and less sweet than a regular tomato. After you peel the husk off a tomatillo, the surface will be a little sticky, so rinse them with a little warm water before using.

If you want a milder salsa (also, see GARTH!!!) simply remove the seeds from the jalapeño and poblano peppers before adding them to the food processor.

BACON STRAWS

I was on The Garth Brooks World Tour (the hubs!) from fall of 2014 through Christmas of 2017. It was a grand adventure with the love of my life. We played multiple shows in one city, so Garth and I would always try to find fun activities to do with the band and crew on a night off or late after the show when you're too excited to go to sleep. One night, after a show in Boston, the founder/executive chairman of Under Armour, Kevin Plank, invited the band and crew to shop after hours in the store. It was a blast! The staff had set up some snacks for us, including these cheesy bacon straws. I tried to be cool and just take one or two, but it was hard not to eat the entire plateful!

SERVES 4 TO 6

¼ cup pure maple syrup

2 teaspoons red pepper flakes

Juice of ½ orange

1 pound regular (not thick-cut) bacon

¼ cup finely grated cheddar cheese

Special Equipment
8 (5-inch) wooden or metal skewers

1   Preheat the oven to 375°F. Fit a rimmed baking sheet with a wire rack.

2   In a small saucepot, whisk together the maple syrup, red pepper flakes, orange juice, and ¼ cup water. Bring to a boil over medium-high heat, stirring continuously, then remove from the heat.

3   Line up the bacon slices on the wire rack and brush them with the hot maple mixture. Sprinkle some cheese on each piece of bacon. With a skewer in hand, fold the end of a piece of bacon in half lengthwise and press the skewer through the end. Do this to 4 pieces of bacon, spreading them out evenly across the skewer, and place the skewer on the baking sheet. Twist the bacon pieces into long spirals so as to create straws. Take another skewer and skewer the bottom of each piece of bacon to keep the bacon twisted. Repeat with all the bacon.

4   Bake until the bacon browns, about 35 minutes. Let cool slightly on the rack. The bacon will get crunchy as it sits. Serve warm or at room temperature.

BAKED GOUDA

with Dried Cherries & Walnuts

We host a holiday party every year and I always try to have some savory snacks to go with all the sweets. This baked Gouda is one of those Instagram-worthy photo finishes because it is just beautiful on the plate, and the bonus is that it looks like it was difficult to make, but it's so easy! My friends also like this party pleaser made with Brie. Try this beautiful cheese round served with my Herbed Crackers (page 193) and apple slices.

SERVES 6 TO 8

1 medium (5- to 6-inch) Gouda cheese round

½ cup cranberry juice

1 tablespoon light brown sugar

½ cup whole dried cherries

½ cup walnuts, toasted and chopped

2 tablespoons honey

¼ teaspoon ground cinnamon

1 (17-ounce) box frozen puff pastry (2 sheets), thawed

1 large egg, lightly beaten, for egg wash

Crackers, for serving

1 Preheat the oven to 350°F.

2 Put the cheese in the freezer to chill for 10 to 15 minutes.

3 In a small saucepan, whisk together the cranberry juice and brown sugar. Bring to a boil over medium-high heat, then turn off the heat and add the cherries. Let the cherries plump for about 10 minutes. Transfer them with a slotted spoon to a medium bowl, add the walnuts, honey, and cinnamon and mix together.

4 **TO ASSEMBLE (SEE PAGES 70-71):** Roll one of the puff pastry sheets with a rolling pin to thin it out. Place the cheese on the center of the pastry. Top the cheese with the cherry-nut mixture. Bring the edges of the pastry to the center and press together. Brush the edges with the egg wash to seal.

5 Cut three 1-inch-wide strips from the remaining puff pastry sheet. Brush with egg wash. Cross the first two strips on top of the pastry-wrapped cheese so they intersect in the center like a ribbon if you were wrapping a present. Coat the edge with egg wash. Form the third strip of puff pastry into a bow shape at the intersection of the first two strips. Place the bow in the center of the cheese and secure with egg wash.

6 Brush the pastry all over with egg wash. Bake until the pastry is light golden brown, about 40 minutes. Let rest for 5 minutes before serving with crackers.

Egg wash gives pastry that shiny, crispy crust that's so beautiful and yummy!

If you can't find a 5- to 6-inch round of Gouda at your grocery store, buy 10 to 12 ounces of Gouda and cut into pieces to form a rough 5- to 6-inch circle.

To reheat leftovers, preheat the oven to 375°F, place the Gouda on a 13 x 18-inch sheet of parchment paper, then fold it over the pastry, tucking it back under. This will protect the cheese from flowing out and the pastry from overbrowning. Bake until heated through, 15 to 20 minutes.

Recipe Continues

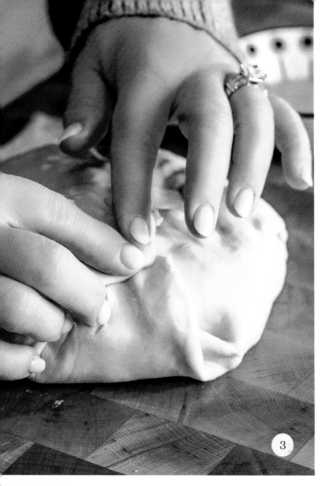

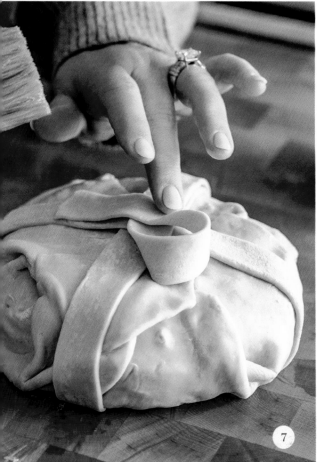

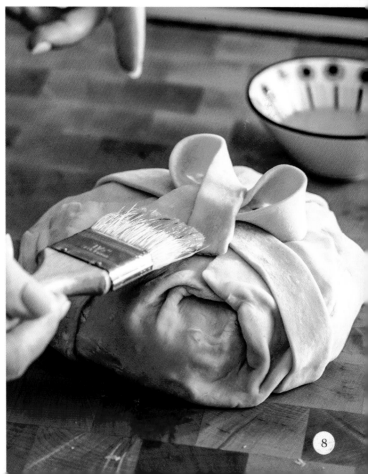

DOUBLE STACKED PORK NACHOS

Germantown, Tennessee, is just a little east of Memphis. There's a BBQ joint there called the Commissary that has just about the best BBQ pork nachos I ever tasted! My friend Julie and I stopped in there for lunch one day on our way to Memphis to visit Graceland. (She'd never been. I've been over a dozen times! I mean . . . Elvis.) I wanted to show Julie all things Memphis, and our first stop was authentic Memphis-style BBQ in Germantown. These nachos were inspired by that meal. I cook a pork shoulder the night before in my slow cooker, so it's ready to go the next day, making these nachos easy to put together. Mixing potato chips with tortilla chips for the bottom layer makes these nachos fit for a king . . . see what I did there? Thank you. Thank you very much!

SERVES 4 TO 6

BBQ Pulled Pork

1½ pounds boneless pork shoulder, cut into large chunks

1½ teaspoons kosher salt

1 teaspoon freshly cracked black pepper

1 teaspoon garlic powder

½ teaspoon ground cumin

½ teaspoon smoked paprika

½ cup apple juice

Barbecue Sauce

2 tablespoons butter

1 small Vidalia onion, chopped

2 garlic cloves, smashed and peeled

¾ cup ketchup

2 tablespoons molasses

2 tablespoons apple cider vinegar

1 tablespoon hot sauce

2 teaspoons Dijon mustard

2 tablespoons pure maple syrup

Cheese Sauce

½ cup heavy cream, plus more if needed

½ teaspoon ground white pepper

6 ounces easy-melting cheese (I like Velveeta), cut into 1-inch chunks

1 (4-ounce) can chopped green chiles, drained

Nachos and Toppings

1 (8-ounce) bag tortilla chips

2 (2-ounce) bags kettle-cooked potato chips

1 (8-ounce) bag grated cheddar cheese (2 cups)

1 small red onion, chopped

3 green onions, sliced into rings

¼ cup sliced pickled jalapeños

1 **MAKE THE PULLED PORK:** Combine the pork chunks, salt, pepper, garlic powder, cumin, and paprika in a 4.5-quart slow cooker. Toss to combine, then pour in the apple juice. Cover and cook on low for 8 hours, or until the pork is easily shredded. Remove the pork from the slow cooker, leaving the juices behind, and place it on a serving dish. Shred the meat with forks or your fingers. Set aside or store in the fridge until ready to use, up to overnight.

2 Preheat the oven to 450°F.

3 **MAKE THE BARBECUE SAUCE:** In a medium saucepan, melt the butter over medium heat. Add the Vidalia onion and cook until tender, about 5 minutes. Add the garlic and cook until the garlic is softened, another 2 to 3 minutes. Add the ketchup, molasses, vinegar, hot sauce, mustard, and maple syrup and simmer until reduced by about ¼ cup, about 5 minutes. Transfer to a blender and carefully blend until smooth.

4 Return the sauce to the pan, add the shredded pork, and warm through over low heat.

5 **MAKE THE CHEESE SAUCE:** In a small saucepan, heat the cream and white pepper over low heat until it just begins to steam, about 3 minutes. Gradually add the melting cheese, stirring until the cheese is completely melted, then add the green chiles. Keep warm, adding a bit more cream if the sauce becomes too thick.

6 **ASSEMBLE THE NACHOS:** In a large bowl, mix the tortilla and potato chips together. In a shallow casserole dish, spread half the tortilla and potato chips, then top with half the BBQ pork and half the grated cheddar, then repeat. Bake until the cheese has melted, 8 to 10 minutes.

7 Pour the cheese sauce over the top and garnish with the red onion, green onions, and pickled jalapeños.

When blending hot liquid, like this barbecue sauce, first let it cool for 5 minutes or so, then transfer it to a blender, filling the blender jar only halfway. Put the lid on, leaving one corner open. Cover the lid with a dish towel to catch splatters and pulse until smooth.

HATCH GREEN CHILE QUESO NACHO BAR

I learned about Hatch chiles when Garth and I played a series of concerts in Las Cruces, New Mexico, on tour in 2017. We brought a case of these chiles home, and I used them in sauces, salsas, and this spicy queso. Hatch chiles are grown in the small town of Hatch, New Mexico, and are considered premium green chiles. They have a very earthy flavor and their heat varies from mild to very hot. If you don't live in New Mexico, you can order them online in whatever level of heat you want, or use Anaheim chiles, which are a good substitute.

SERVES 6 TO 8

1 tablespoon butter

1 large shallot, minced

¼ teaspoon kosher salt

¼ teaspoon ground cumin

½ teaspoon chili powder

4 teaspoons cornstarch

1 (12-ounce) can evaporated milk

3 (4-ounce) cans diced hot or mild Hatch green chiles

8 ounces mild cheddar cheese, grated

8 ounces white American cheese, chopped into small pieces

Fixings

Tortilla chips

Diced plum tomatoes

Sliced pickled jalapeños

Sliced olives

Chopped green onions

Diced avocado

1 bunch cilantro, chopped

1. In a medium saucepan, melt the butter over medium-low heat, then add the shallots, salt, cumin, and chili powder and cook until the shallots are softened and fragrant, about 5 minutes.

2. In a small bowl, stir together the cornstarch and 1 tablespoon of the evaporated milk to make a slurry; set aside.

3. Stir the green chiles and the remaining evaporated milk into the pot and bring just to a simmer, then stir in the cornstarch slurry and both cheeses. Stir until the cheeses have melted and the mixture is combined. Cook over low heat for 3 to 4 minutes, until thick and creamy. You want to be able to drizzle the queso over the tortilla chips but have it be thick enough to stay on the chips.

4. To serve, transfer the queso to a slow cooker set on low and have all the fixings set up for friends to create their own personal little platters of nachos.

TRISHA'S TIP

What's a slurry, you ask? Ever added a little flour or cornstarch to a recipe to thicken the batter—only to have it stay in little chunks and become almost impossible to stir in? Dissolving the flour or cornstarch into a little liquid creates what is called a slurry, which allows you to add a dry ingredient smoothly.

SWEET BUTTER PUFFCORN

This is one of those snacks that you have to taste to believe. It's so incredibly simple, but you HAVE to know about it! Almond bark is really just a chocolate-like confection that sets faster than chocolate (think candy coating or candy melts). I use the vanilla flavor in this recipe, but use the chocolate flavor if you prefer. The combination of this vanilla candy coating with the buttery puffcorn is the ultimate salty-sweet snack combo. My Oklahoma friend Marcia first made this treat for me and brought it to a Zumba class we both attended. You may need to do an extra exercise class after eating this salty-sweet goodness, but . . . it's worth it!

SERVES 8

1 (1-pound) package vanilla-flavored almond bark or candy coating (like Candiquik)

2 (3.5-ounce) bags butter puffcorn (I like Chester's)

1   Melt the almond bark in a medium microwave-safe bowl in 30-second increments until completely melted and smooth, 1 to 2 minutes.

2   Place the puffcorn in a large bowl. Pour the melted almond bark over the puffcorn and gently mix until the puffcorn is completely coated.

3   Spread the mixture out over a sheet of parchment paper in a single layer and let set, about 10 minutes. Store in an airtight container at room temperature for up to 2 weeks.

TRISHA'S TIP

If the puffcorn is left uncovered, it will get soggy, so keep a lid on it!

EVERYTHING BAGEL DIP

We've all had those amazing "everything" bagels. You can now buy this spice blend premade, but making your own is so simple. If you have any left over, store it in your pantry to sprinkle over your morning cream cheese–topped bagel. I suggest adding 2 tablespoons to the dip, but you can be more generous with it for more of that tasty everything-bagel flavor!

SERVES 4 TO 6

2 tablespoons poppy seeds

2 tablespoons white sesame seeds

1 tablespoon black sesame seeds

1 tablespoon dried minced garlic

1 tablespoon dried minced onion

1 tablespoon coarse kosher salt

2 (8-ounce) packages cream cheese, at room temperature

¼ cup hot pepper jelly, store-bought or try my Spicy Red Pepper Jelly (page 205), plus more for serving

1 (7-ounce) bag bagel chips, for serving

1   In a small bowl, combine the poppy seeds, white sesame seeds, black sesame seeds, garlic, onion, and salt. Transfer 2 tablespoons of the mixture to a food processor. Add the cream cheese and pepper jelly to the food processor and pulse until completely combined.

2   Transfer the mixture to a small serving bowl and sprinkle with more spice mix and a couple of dollops of pepper jelly. Serve with the bagel chips. Store the remaining spice mix in an airtight container for another use.

This dip can be made a few days ahead of time and kept in an airtight container in the refrigerator until ready to serve.

STEAK & AVOCADO ROLLS

This take on avocado rolls comes from our girls' love of sushi. Garth and I would often take them to their favorite restaurant in Tulsa, In the Raw. Taylor, August, and Allie would order everything from tuna to octopus. Garth and I would always order rice bowls and avocado rolls. We continue to steer clear of raw fish! When we re-create our In the Raw experience at home, I pair these steak and avocado rolls with Garth's Teriyaki Bowl (page 116). These rolls are not quite as fancy as the foods the girls eat, but they're as close to sushi as this chick singer and her cowboy are gonna get!

SERVES 4

1 (8-ounce) boneless rib eye steak

2 tablespoons olive oil

1 teaspoon freshly ground black pepper

1¼ teaspoons kosher salt

1 cup panko bread crumbs

1 teaspoon black sesame seeds

½ cup mayonnaise

2 tablespoons sriracha

6 to 8 (10-inch) square soy sushi wrappers

1 avocado, sliced

1 yellow bell pepper, julienned or very thinly sliced

1   Heat a large cast-iron skillet over medium-high heat and add olive oil. Sprinkle the steak with the pepper and 1 teaspoon of the salt, and cook for about 5 minutes per side, until medium. Transfer the steak to a cutting board and let rest for 7 minutes.

2   Meanwhile, reduce the heat under the skillet to medium and add the panko, sesame seeds, and remaining ¼ teaspoon salt. Cook, stirring frequently, until the panko is golden brown. Transfer to a bowl and set aside to cool.

3   Slice the steak into thin strips. In a medium bowl, mix the mayonnaise and sriracha and set aside.

4   Place a soy wrapper in front of you on a clean workspace. On the wrapper edge closest to you, spread a thin line of the spicy mayo. Lay down 2 avocado slices, lengthwise, touching each other. Stack a few pepper slices so that the entire edge is covered in a layer of peppers. Spread another thin layer of spicy mayo over the peppers, then sprinkle 2 tablespoons of the panko mixture over them. Add a few slices of steak on top of the panko. Carefully roll the wrapper away from you to enclose the filling, creating a thin tube. Add another thin line of spicy mayo to the outer edge of the wrapper to help you seal the roll. Set the tube aside and repeat with the remaining wrappers and filling ingredients. Cut each roll crosswise into 1½-inch-wide slices. Place the rolls on a serving plate and enjoy.

Trisha's Tip

If you have a medium squeeze bottle, put the mayo and sriracha in the bottle and shake until combined. A resealable bag or piping bag would also work well to evenly squeeze a small line of spicy mayo onto the soy wrapper.

BUFFALO CHICKEN DIP

Buffalo wings have become one of the most popular appetizers in the country. Dipping that almost-too-hot wing into the coolness of a sour cream or ranch dip is heavenly! The only complaint I have is that it takes a lot of little wings to fill you up, and we all know what a mess it is to eat them. I decided to turn that awesomeness into a dip. Oh, and that sour cream that's usually served on the side for your wings? It's INSIDE the dip!

SERVES 4 TO 6

---

6 tablespoons (¾ stick) butter

1 medium onion, diced

2 boneless, skinless chicken breasts, thinly sliced

3 garlic cloves, minced

⅔ cup cayenne hot sauce (I like Louisiana hot sauce)

½ cup sour cream

½ cup mayonnaise

1 cup grated cheddar cheese

¾ cup blue cheese crumbles

3 green onions, thinly sliced

3 carrots, cut into sticks, for serving

4 celery stalks, cut into sticks, for serving

Tortilla chips, for serving

1   In a large skillet with a lid, melt 2 tablespoons of the butter over medium heat. Add the onion and cook until translucent, about 5 minutes.

2   Add the chicken, garlic, hot sauce, 2 tablespoons water, and the remaining 4 tablespoons (½ stick) butter and bring to a simmer. Cover the pan and reduce the heat to low. Cook for 45 minutes to 1 hour, until the chicken is falling apart and the sauce has reduced to almost dry.

3   Preheat the broiler.

4   Break apart the chicken into small pieces with the back of a spoon. Add the sour cream, mayonnaise, cheddar, and ¼ cup of the blue cheese to the pan with the chicken and stir until well combined and heated through. Transfer the dip to an ovenproof serving dish and broil until it bubbles and starts to brown, 3 to 4 minutes.

5   Top with the green onions and remaining ½ cup blue cheese. Serve with the carrots, celery, and tortilla chips.

GREEN GODDESS DIP

I am old enough to remember the Wish-Bone Green Goddess salad dressing commercials on TV in the '70s, but I was surprised to learn the dressing originated long before that! In the early 1920s, there was a hit play running in San Francisco called *The Green Goddess*. The lead actor, George Arliss, was staying at the Palace Hotel, and the hotel chef was inspired to make a dressing in his honor. But even that chef wasn't the first guy to make this beautiful green concoction! His version was inspired by a dressing that came out of Louis XIII's palace kitchens, though that one wasn't served on salads, but with eel. (Ew.) I've turned this over-500-year-old dressing into a light, creamy, and, yes, beautifully green, dip that's fit for a king . . . or a goddess!

SERVES 4 TO 6

1½ cups fresh parsley leaves

1 cup fresh mint leaves

½ cup fresh basil leaves

1 bunch chives, chopped (about ¼ cup)

½ cup sour cream

¼ cup mayonnaise

Zest and juice of 1 lemon (about 2 tablespoons juice)

1 (8-ounce) package cream cheese, at room temperature

½ teaspoon kosher salt, plus more if needed

¼ teaspoon freshly ground black pepper, plus more if needed

Sliced fresh vegetables and potato chips, for serving

1 In a food processor, combine the parsley, mint, basil, chives, sour cream, mayonnaise, lemon zest, lemon juice, cream cheese, salt, and pepper and process for 3 minutes, stopping and scraping down the sides to make sure all the ingredients are fully incorporated. Taste and add more salt and pepper, if needed.

2 Transfer to a bowl. Serve with sliced fresh vegetables and potato chips for dipping.

Buffalo
Chicken Dip
80

Green
Goddess
Dip
81

Caramelized
Onion
Bacon Dip
84

CARAMELIZED ONION BACON DIP

Caramelized onions are great served as a topping on pizza, or on a greasy cheeseburger, but I especially love them in this warm, cheesy dip. Combined with crispy thick-cut bacon and three different cheeses, this dip will go fast. I don't give any tips on storing leftovers, because I guarantee you won't have any!

SERVES 6 TO 8

4 slices thick-cut bacon

2 large sweet onions (I like Vidalia), halved, then thinly sliced into half-moons

½ teaspoon garlic powder

1 teaspoon dry mustard powder

1 teaspoon kosher salt

¼ teaspoon freshly cracked black pepper

½ (8-ounce) package cream cheese, at room temperature

¼ cup plain Greek yogurt

2 tablespoons mayonnaise

1 teaspoon Worcestershire sauce

⅔ cup grated sharp cheddar cheese

⅔ cup grated Swiss cheese

2 tablespoons chopped fresh chives, plus 1 tablespoon for garnish

Sliced fresh veggies and a sliced baguette, for serving

1   Preheat the oven to 375°F. Fit a rimmed baking sheet with a wire rack.

2   Place the bacon on the rack and bake for 20 to 25 minutes, until crispy.

3   Pour the bacon fat from the pan into a large skillet and warm over medium-high heat. Add the onions to the skillet and cook, stirring frequently, for about 1 minute. Sprinkle in the garlic powder, mustard powder, ½ teaspoon salt, and the pepper, then reduce the heat to medium-low and cook until the onions are browned, soft, and caramelized, 40 to 45 minutes. Set aside.

4   In a medium bowl, stir together the cream cheese, yogurt, mayonnaise, and Worcestershire until smooth and combined. Add the cheddar, Swiss cheese, remaining ½ teaspoon salt, and 2 tablespoons of the chives and stir until completely combined. Stir in the warm caramelized onions. Crumble the bacon and stir it into the dip.

5   Transfer the dip to a serving bowl and sprinkle with the remaining 1 tablespoon chives. Serve warm, with fresh veggies and a sliced baguette.

TRISHA'S TIP

Caramelizing onions is a long, drawn-out yet simple process that's totally worth the end result. Don't rush it, and you'll have sweet, creamy onions when you're done.

WALNUT PESTO PINWHEELS

Instead of the traditional pine nuts used in most pesto sauces, I like to use walnuts. They are milder in flavor, but still pack a punch. Pesto isn't just for pasta! I love it on toast, and I even use it for the sauce on pizza in place of red sauce. Rolling this flavorful pesto into tender puff pastry and topping with Parmesan cheese is a great way to serve it. I make these for appetizers on nights when I know supper is going to take a little longer to cook. I never have leftovers!

SERVES 6 TO 8

¼ cup walnuts

¼ cup extra-virgin olive oil

⅓ cup grated Parmesan cheese, plus more for sprinkling

1 tablespoon fresh lemon juice

2 garlic cloves, smashed and peeled

Kosher salt

2 cups fresh basil, roughly chopped

1 egg

1 (17-ounce) box frozen puff pastry, thawed

¼ cup jarred pizza sauce, for serving

1 Preheat the oven to 375°F, with racks in the upper and lower thirds. Line two baking sheets with parchment paper.

2 In a food processor, combine the walnuts and the olive oil and process until smooth, about 1 minute. Add the Parmesan, lemon juice, garlic, and ½ teaspoon salt and process until blended, about 1 minute. Add the basil and process until smooth.

3 In a small bowl, whisk together the egg and 1 teaspoon water to make an egg wash.

4 Lay out one of the puff pastry sheets with one of the longer sides closest to you. Using a rolling pin, roll it out a little in all directions to smooth out the fold lines, taking care to not over-roll. Spoon a thin layer of the pesto over the pastry, avoiding the last ½ inch of the edge farthest away from you. Tightly roll the pastry away from you, brushing the last ½ inch with some egg wash, then press that edge against the roll, making a nice log. Wrap it in plastic wrap, put it in the freezer, and repeat with the remaining sheet of pastry. Chill the filled pastry rolls for about 10 minutes, so they will be firm enough to slice cleanly.

5 With a sharp knife, slice the rolls crosswise into ½-inch-wide wheels and lay them out on the prepared baking sheets. Brush all the wheels with the egg wash and bake for 18 to 20 minutes, until golden brown, switching the pans (top and bottom) and rotating them 180 degrees for even cooking.

6 Remove the pinwheels from the oven, sprinkle with Parmesan, and let cool on the pans for 5 minutes before transferring to a serving platter. Serve with the sauce, at room temperature or warmed.

Walnut
Pesto
Pinwheels
85

BLUE CRAB & LEMON PEPPER RANCH TOASTS

I've often talked about growing up in a small town in middle Georgia, where the only fish we ate were catfish and bream that we caught fresh in the pond on our farm. I loved it! Any time I tried any kind of shellfish at a restaurant, it had been flown or trucked in from the coast, so it was never super fresh, and I made up my mind early that I didn't like it. On a trip to Ocean City, Maryland, on tour in the early '90s, I sat overlooking the Atlantic Ocean and ordered fresh crab for the first time. Wow! I had no idea what I had been missing. Even though Nashville isn't on the coast, it's a big city, so there are several really good fish markets where I can find the fresh lump crabmeat I want for these lemony ranch crab toasts. I love to serve these at brunch with my gal pals.

SERVES 6 TO 8

Lemon Pepper Ranch

½ cup mayonnaise

¼ cup sour cream

Zest of 1 lemon

2 teaspoons fresh lemon juice

½ teaspoon kosher salt

1¼ teaspoons freshly ground black pepper

¼ teaspoon garlic powder

¼ teaspoon onion powder

1 teaspoon dried parsley

½ teaspoon dried dill

Pinch of cayenne pepper

Crab Salad

12 slices sturdy white bread (day-old bread works great)

8 ounces lump crabmeat

4 tablespoons (½ stick) sweet cream butter (see Tips)

1 garlic clove, smashed

2 tablespoons chopped fresh parsley leaves, plus torn leaves for garnish

2 tablespoons finely chopped fresh dill

1 tablespoon finely chopped pepperoncini (seeds and stem discarded), plus 1 teaspoon liquid from the jar

2 celery stalks, finely diced

Kosher salt

1 Preheat the oven to 400°F. Set a baking sheet on the middle rack to preheat.

2 MAKE THE LEMON PEPPER RANCH: In a small bowl, mix the mayonnaise, sour cream, lemon zest, lemon juice, salt, black pepper, garlic powder, onion powder, parsley, dill, and cayenne and set aside.

3 MAKE THE CRAB SALAD: Trim the crusts off the bread slices and cut each slice in half into triangles. Place on the preheated baking sheet and toast until just beginning to lightly brown, about 4 minutes. Remove from the oven and let cool.

4 Put the crabmeat in a medium bowl and pick through it for any shell pieces. In a small saucepan, stir together the butter and garlic. Cook over low heat for 30 seconds, until the butter has melted and the garlic is fragrant. The butter will foam but should not brown.

5 Remove the garlic and pour the melted butter over the crab, stirring it through. Add the parsley, dill, pepperoncini and its liquid, celery, and a pinch of salt and stir. Taste and add more salt if needed.

6 When you're ready to serve, line up the toasts and spread a nice layer of the ranch over them all, then top each toast with about 1 tablespoon of the crab salad. Finish by adding a few torn parsley leaves on the top of each. Serve warm.

Sweet cream butter is butter made from fresh cream. Its name does not mean it's sweet. Regular butter is made with sour cream and is a little tangy. Either works in this crab salad, but I love the creaminess of sweet cream butter.

If a banana pepper and a hot pepper had a baby, it would be a pepperoncini. This pepper combines the best of both! Use jarred pepperoncini in this recipe so you'll have the juice from the jar to use in the salad.

OVEN BEEF JERKY, TWO WAYS

Garth and I are beef jerky connoisseurs. Whether it's the packaged varieties we get at the grocery store or the special homemade gifts from friends, we just love it. I never made it myself, because I didn't want to go to the trouble. I thought I needed special equipment for the whole process, until I discovered that I could actually turn my oven into a slow dehydrator! This long-and-slow oven method will have you making your own beef jerky all the time. It's SO easy, and SO tasty. The BBQ and teriyaki flavors are two of our favorites.

BBQ Marinade

½ cup ketchup

½ cup packed light brown sugar

½ cup apple cider vinegar

2 tablespoons Worcestershire sauce

2 teaspoons kosher salt

1 teaspoon garlic powder

1 teaspoon paprika

Teriyaki Marinade

1 cup soy sauce

½ cup light brown sugar, packed

2 tablespoons sriracha

1 tablespoon Worcestershire sauce

1 teaspoon garlic powder

1 teaspoon ground ginger

Juice of 1 lime (about 2 tablespoons)

1½ pounds beef top round, placed in the freezer for 30 minutes

1 **TO MAKE THE BBQ MARINADE:** In a large resealable bag, stir together the ketchup, brown sugar, vinegar, Worcestershire, salt, garlic powder, and paprika.

2 **TO MAKE THE TERIYAKI MARINADE:** In a large resealable bag, stir together the soy sauce, brown sugar, sriracha, Worcestershire, garlic powder, ginger, and lime juice.

3 Thinly slice the partially frozen meat against the grain. Place the meat in the bag with the marinade, seal, and coat all the pieces. Marinate in the refrigerator for at least 4 hours or up to overnight.

4 Preheat the oven to 200°F. Line two rimmed baking sheets with aluminum foil and set a wire rack on top of each pan.

5 Lay the slices of meat flat on the racks in a single layer. Bake until the jerky is completely dried, 3½ to 4 hours. Store in airtight containers at room temperature for up to 2 weeks.

TRISHA'S TIP

Putting the meat in the freezer for 30 minutes helps it firm up just enough to make slicing easier. You can skip this step and ask your butcher to slice the beef for you, if you like.

Oven Beef Jerky

ROASTED CHICKPEA SNACKS

Chickpeas, also called garbanzo beans, are really magical additions to recipes for me. I love them crushed up and added to veggie burgers, tossed in a salad for extra protein, or roasted like these for a snack. The great thing about roasting chickpeas is that you can flavor them a million different ways! I like chili powder for a little heat, but you can add any spices you like, sweet or savory. I laugh when I think about the note for storing up to a week . . . these snacks never make it through the day at my house!

SERVES 6

2 (15-ounce) cans chickpeas, drained and rinsed

2 tablespoons olive oil

1 teaspoon kosher salt

½ teaspoon freshly ground black pepper

1 tablespoon hot Mexican-style chili powder

1 Preheat the oven to 450°F. Line a large baking sheet with aluminum foil.

2 Using paper towels or a clean dish towel, pat the chickpeas dry. In a large bowl, toss the chickpeas with the olive oil, salt, and pepper. Spread the chickpeas evenly over the prepared baking sheet. Bake for 30 to 40 minutes, stirring every 10 minutes, until brown and crispy. Remove from the oven and toss with the chili powder.

3 Allow the chickpeas to cool before storing in an airtight container at room temperature for up to 1 week. Eat as a snack or toss in your favorite salad.

Roasted Chickpeas

TRISHA's TIPS

Toss with the chili powder AFTER taking the chickpeas out of the oven. Baking can cause spices to burn and taste bitter.

As the chickpeas cool, they become chewier and less crunchy. Both ways taste great.

PIZZA-PASTA SNACK MIX

This tasty snack mix is for cooks who want to seriously up their appetizer game! I don't fry that much anymore, so I double this recipe and store any leftovers in the refrigerator for up to two weeks. It usually doesn't last that long! *Orecchiette* is Italian for "little ears," which refers to the shape of the pasta. Frying up these little pasta ears along with the pepperoni gives this snack the perfect crunch.

SERVES 4

1 quart vegetable oil, for frying

¼ cup grated Parmesan cheese

1 teaspoon Italian seasoning

¼ teaspoon garlic powder

¼ teaspoon red pepper flakes

2 cups orecchiette pasta, cooked (see Tips)

Kosher salt

2 ounces packaged pepperoni slices, cut into quarters

8 sun-dried tomatoes, chopped into small pieces

1   Pour the oil into a medium Dutch oven or heavy-bottomed pan. Clip a deep-fry thermometer to its side and heat the oil over medium-high heat to 375°F. Line a baking sheet with paper towels and set it nearby.

2   In a small bowl, mix together the Parmesan, Italian seasoning, garlic powder, and red pepper flakes. Set aside.

3   Fry half the pasta in the hot oil until lightly golden brown, 2 to 3 minutes, flipping it gently as it cooks. The orecchiette might stick together a little, but will break apart as it cools. Transfer the pasta with a large slotted spoon to the paper towel–lined baking sheet and sprinkle with salt. Allow the oil to return to 375°F and repeat with the remaining pasta.

4   Allow the temperature of the oil to drop to 360°F, then quickly fry the pepperoni for 1 minute. Transfer to a paper towel–lined plate to cool. Turn the heat off under the oil.

5   Once the fried pasta and pepperoni are cool enough to handle, transfer them to a large metal or heat-safe glass bowl. Add the sun-dried tomatoes and the Parmesan blend and toss three or four times, then carefully add a tablespoon of the hot frying oil and toss to coat everything completely. Serve warm.

When preparing pasta to fry, first cook it according to the package directions, then drain it and lay it out on a parchment-lined baking sheet. Toss with 1 tablespoon oil and let cool. Be sure there's no residual water on the pasta before frying by patting dry with a paper towel.

If you're serving this snack later, let the mix cool completely and then store in an airtight container in the fridge.

COLLARD-STUFFED WONTONS

Anybody who knows me knows that collards are my favorite greens. I'm always looking for ways to serve them. Other than my traditional childhood method of spooning over fresh cornbread (yum), I have used them in very nontraditional ways, in place of grape leaves for Mediterranean dolmas, sweetened with brown sugar for a crispy side, and even mixed into a grits casserole! I use Instant Pot–braised collards for these wontons. If you don't do spicy, just use regular honey in the sweet dipping sauce. You can substitute a different leafy green in these wontons, but I promise you've never tasted a collard green like this!

◆

SERVES 6 TO 8

Hot Honey Pimento Sauce

¼ cup hot honey

1 teaspoon apple cider vinegar

2 tablespoons pureed pimentos

2 teaspoons cornstarch

Wontons

1 quart vegetable oil, for frying

1 cup Instant Pot Collard Greens (page 103), drained and roughly chopped

1 (8-ounce) package cream cheese, at room temperature

¼ teaspoon freshly ground black pepper

32 square wonton wrappers

1   **MAKE THE SAUCE:** In a small saucepan, mix together the honey, vinegar, and pimentos over low heat. In a small bowl, stir together 1 tablespoon water and the cornstarch until the cornstarch dissolves, creating a slurry. Add the slurry to the honey mixture, stir, and simmer until the sauce thickens, about 5 minutes. Set aside. As the sauce cools, it will thicken even more.

2   **MAKE THE WONTONS:** Pour the oil into a heavy-bottomed medium Dutch oven (it should come about 1½ inches up the sides). Clip a deep-fry thermometer to its side and heat the oil over high heat to 350°F. Fit a wire rack over a rimmed baking sheet and set it nearby.

3   While the oil is heating up, in a medium bowl, combine the collards, cream cheese, and pepper and whip using a hand mixer until combined, about 1 minute.

4   Fill a small bowl with a few tablespoons of water and lay out half the wonton wrappers on a clean surface. Add about ¾ tablespoon of the cream cheese filling to just the side of the center of each wrapper. Dip your fingertip in the water and wet the edges of one wrapper all the way around, then fold over into a triangle and press the edges together. Set aside and repeat with the remaining wrappers and filling.

5   Working in batches of about 6, fry the wontons in the hot oil for 1 to 2 minutes, until they are a light golden brown, using a slotted spoon to flip them to cook both sides. Transfer the wontons with the slotted spoon to the rack to drain and cool slightly. Repeat to fry the remaining wontons.

6   Serve the wontons with the hot honey pimento sauce for dipping.

BREAD-AND-BUTTER PICKLE BRINED WINGS

Chicken wings are a food group for my friend Glenda. I think she would eat them every day if she could, and when they're this good, why wouldn't you? You'll love the pickle-y brine on these wings. I like the baby drumsticks and Glenda likes the flats, so we're a good pair when it comes to wing eating. I make these wings for Glenda every year instead of a birthday cake!

◆

SERVES 4

3 pounds chicken wings, tips removed, split (see Tip)

1 (24-ounce) jar bread-and-butter pickles

Kosher salt and freshly ground black pepper

3 tablespoons butter

½ cup honey mustard

¼ cup hot sauce (I like Tabasco)

1 Place the chicken wings into a gallon-size resealable bag. Drain the brine from the jar of pickles into the bag and add 1 cup water, or enough to just cover the wings. Carefully let the air out of the bag while you zip it to ensure that the wings are fully submerged. Brine in the fridge for at least 3 hours or up to overnight.

2 Preheat the oven to 400°F, with racks in the upper and lower thirds. Line two large rimmed baking sheets with parchment paper.

3 Drain the wings and blot them with a paper towel to dry them a little. Divide the wings between the prepared pans and sprinkle with salt and pepper. Arrange them skin-side up and roast until the skin is golden brown and crispy, 25 to 30 minutes, rotating the pans halfway through.

4 Meanwhile, in a medium saucepan, melt the butter over medium heat. Whisk in the honey mustard and hot sauce, season with pepper, reduce the heat to low, and cook for 3 to 4 minutes.

5 Transfer the wings to a large bowl and toss with the sauce, then place on a serving platter.

 TRISHA'S TIP

To remove the tip on a wing, hold a sharp knife at the center of the joint, and cut through at the top end of the tip. To section the drummie from the flat (or paddle), slice at the joint and separate the two pieces.

LEMON BASIL BRUSCHETTA

There's nothing better than a little crunchy baguette square topped with salty goodness to start off a meal. Whenever I'm out to dinner, I always go for the bruschetta as an appetizer because it gives me the satisfaction of a little bite of bread with yummy toppings, and keeps me from eating the whole bread basket before the meal comes! I've taken this idea and come up with these crunchy, tomato-topped bites that keep my guests happy and satisfied while I'm finishing up supper.

SERVES 4 TO 6

2 cups mixed-color grape tomatoes, quartered

¾ cup finely chopped orange bell pepper

1 tablespoon finely chopped fresh basil

½ garlic clove, finely grated

¼ teaspoon Old Bay seasoning

2 tablespoons olive oil

¼ teaspoon kosher salt

Freshly ground black pepper

1 lemon

1 baguette, sliced and lightly toasted, for serving

In a medium bowl, gently toss the tomatoes, bell pepper, basil, garlic, Old Bay, olive oil, salt, and a few grinds of black pepper. Zest 1 teaspoon of lemon zest over the bowl so some of those awesome lemon oils spray in as you zest, and stir to combine. Serve with toasted baguette slices.

Change this bruschetta up by using your favorite fresh herbs. Try it with any kind of fresh basil, oregano, or summer savory.

ROASTED SWEET POTATO HUMMUS

One of my go-to sides for dinner is almost always a large sheet pan full of roasted root vegetables. You really can't go wrong with them, no matter what you're serving. I notice that I almost always pick out the almost-caramelized, deep-orange sweet potatoes first, because I love the flavor. I turned my favorite roasted root vegetable into an easy hummus that everyone loves. The richness of the roasted sweet potato is truly satisfying!

SERVES 12

3 medium sweet potatoes

3 garlic cloves, peeled

1 (15-ounce) can chickpeas, drained and rinsed

3 tablespoons tahini

⅓ cup fresh lemon juice

½ teaspoon smoked paprika, plus more for sprinkling

½ teaspoon ground cumin

1 teaspoon kosher salt, plus more as needed

¼ teaspoon freshly ground black pepper, plus more as needed

7 tablespoons olive oil, plus more for drizzling

Cut fresh veggies and pita chips, for serving

1 Preheat the oven to 425°F. Line a baking sheet with parchment paper or aluminum foil.

2 Pierce the skin of the sweet potatoes 3 or 4 times with the tip of a paring knife. Put them on the prepared baking sheet and bake for 40 to 50 minutes, until a paring knife goes in smoothly. Remove from the oven and let cool slightly.

3 When the sweet potatoes are cool enough to hold, peel off the skin with your hands; it will come away easily. Place the sweet potato flesh in a medium bowl and mash lightly with a fork. You should have about 3 cups mashed flesh.

4 In a food processor, combine the garlic and chickpeas and pulse to break them up a little, then add the mashed sweet potato, tahini, lemon juice, paprika, cumin, salt, and pepper and puree until fully combined. With the processor running on low and the tube on the lid open, slowly drizzle in the olive oil, 1 tablespoon at a time, to incorporate. Taste and season with salt and pepper.

5 Transfer the hummus to a medium serving bowl and top with a drizzle of olive oil and a sprinkle of smoked paprika. Serve with veggies and pita chips for dipping.

Soups, Salads & Sides

I've never thought of soups or salads as "starters,"
but dishes that could be served as entrées, too. I feel the same
way about sides, so you'll find hearty options in this section.
You'll also discover new ways to make old favorites like Instant Pot
collard greens, and twists on Southern classics like
potato salad. Everything here serves as a tasty opener for a
great meal, or as a lunch or dinner on its own.

INSTANT POT COLLARD GREENS

My dad planted rows and rows of collards in our garden when I was a kid. We had so much yield that he would invite friends and neighbors to drive up and help themselves to what they wanted. Most kids had to be coaxed into eating their greens, but not me! I could eat collards every day and be a happy camper. The only thing I never liked about greens is how long they took to cook down, and how they smelled up the house. This Instant Pot magic gets rid of both issues!

SERVES 6

¼ pound bacon, cut into ½-inch pieces

1½ teaspoons kosher salt

¼ teaspoon freshly ground black pepper

1 large sweet onion (I like Vidalia), halved and thinly sliced

4 garlic cloves, minced

¼ cup apple cider vinegar

2 tablespoons honey

½ teaspoon red pepper flakes

2 bunches collard greens, ribs removed and leaves cut into 2-inch-wide strips

¾ cup chicken stock

Hot Honey Cornbread (page 192), for serving

1 In an Instant Pot set to Sauté, combine the bacon, salt, and black pepper and sauté for 6 minutes. Add the onion and sauté for 4 minutes more. Add the garlic and stir until fragrant, about 1 minute.

2 Add the vinegar and deglaze the pot, scraping up any browned bits with a wooden spoon, then let the liquid reduce for about 2 minutes. Stir in the honey and red pepper flakes.

3 Add the collard greens and chicken stock and stir. Secure the lid on the Instant Pot, select Manual, and set to cook on high pressure for 5 minutes. Allow the pressure to release naturally for 20 minutes, then manually release the remaining pressure.

4 Serve the collards over hot honey cornbread.

Trisha's Tips

If the collards don't all fit into the Instant Pot, add half the greens with the chicken stock to soften and cook down a little, then add the rest to the pot. They will all fit, promise!

Use leftovers in Collard-Stuffed Wontons (page 94).

JANET'S POTATO SALAD

My go-to favorite potato salad has always been my mama's basic mayo-and-sweet-relish version. Until now. Wow! My friend Janet suggested I try her twist on my mom's classic, and it's so good I know Gwen would approve! Janet is an authentic Louisiana Cajun Southern belle. Her family came from France to Louisiana in the 1700s and has been there ever since. She serves this potato salad at family dinners, and everyone has come to count on it. I love it because it combines everything I enjoy about my mom's original recipe, with the wonderful surprise of an apple crunch. Janet says the addition of apple was to help make a cooling side to balance spicy dishes like jambalaya, gumbo, or shrimp creole. All I can say is, *Ça c'est bon!* (That's good!)

SERVES 8

3 pounds red potatoes, cut into ½-inch cubes

1½ teaspoons kosher salt

1 cup mayonnaise

¼ cup yellow mustard

⅓ cup sweet pickle relish

½ teaspoon freshly ground black pepper

½ teaspoon sweet paprika, plus more for garnish

1 large Granny Smith apple

4 large hard-boiled eggs, peeled and diced

2 tablespoons thinly sliced fresh chives, for garnish

1 Place the potatoes in a large saucepan or pressure cooker (see Tip). Sprinkle the potatoes with ½ teaspoon of the salt and add enough water to cover the potatoes. Boil for 30 minutes, or until the potatoes are tender when pierced with the point of a knife but still hold their shape. Drain, transfer to a large bowl, and let cool completely.

2 While the potatoes cool, in a small bowl, mix together the mayonnaise, mustard, relish, the remaining 1 teaspoon of salt, pepper, and paprika.

3 Peel, core, and dice the apple into ½-inch pieces and add it to the bowl with the cooled potatoes. Add the mayonnaise mixture and stir to combine. Fold in the diced eggs. Cover and chill in the refrigerator for at least 1 hour or up to overnight.

4 Sprinkle a little more paprika and the chives over the top just before serving.

To cook the potatoes in a pressure cooker, sprinkle the salt over the potatoes and follow the manufacturer's instructions to cook on high pressure for 5 minutes. Release the pressure immediately, then drain and cool the potatoes.

Make this potato salad leaving the skin on the potatoes, or peel them before dicing if you prefer. Either way, it's so tasty!

CRISPY RICE CORN FRITTERS

I came up with these crispy rice-and-corn beauties as the answer for a frequent leftover in our house: rice. Garth loves rice in everything, from steak and chicken bowls to smothered in gravy as a side to Sunday roast. I usually make a lot so we don't run out. As a result, I have cold rice to contend with. You can reheat cold rice by putting a little water in it and microwaving it for about 30 seconds, but these rice-and-corn fritters are a much better use for that leftover sticky white rice! We love these fritters dipped in my Green Goddess Dip (page 81).

◆

MAKES 12 FRITTERS

2 cups cooked white rice, cooled or cold

4 green onions, sliced into ¼-inch rounds

1 cup fresh or frozen sweet corn kernels, thawed if frozen

4 ounces cheddar cheese, grated (1 cup)

3 tablespoons diced pimentos, drained

12 large basil leaves, sliced into thin ribbons

4 large eggs

1 teaspoon sweet paprika

1 teaspoon kosher salt, plus more as needed

¼ teaspoon freshly ground black pepper

Vegetable oil, for frying

Sour cream, for serving

1   In a medium bowl, stir together the rice, green onions, corn, cheddar, pimentos, and basil. In another medium bowl, whisk together the eggs, paprika, salt, and pepper, then pour over the rice mixture and stir to combine. Let the mixture sit for 5 minutes.

2   Meanwhile, fill a large cast-iron skillet with ¼ inch of oil and heat the oil over medium high heat until it shimmers. Line a baking sheet with paper towels and set it nearby.

3   Scoop ¼ cup of the rice mixture, pressing it down lightly in the measuring cup, then turn it out into the hot oil and lightly flatten it. (You can cook 3 or 4 at a time, depending on the size of your skillet.) Fry for 1½ to 2 minutes, until browned underneath. Take care to not move the fritters around after you first add them to the pan, so they stay intact while they cook. Gently flip the fritters and cook for another 2 to 2½ minutes. Transfer to the paper towel–lined baking sheet to drain and sprinkle with a bit of salt while warm. Serve with a dollop of sour cream.

If you are making fresh white rice for this recipe, let it cool completely, or even store it in the fridge overnight, before using it to make the fritters. Leftover rice will stick together better for frying than freshly cooked.

KAT'S ARANCINI

One of the advantages of having a neighbor who is a great cook is that she drops off little covered plates of awesomeness on a weekly basis! My friend Kathy never comes to visit empty-handed. She's always bringing something sweet she made, or some kind of homemade bread for us to enjoy. Sometimes she will just drop off a meal for us, and it's always tasty, and frequently Italian, as that's her heritage. We were the lucky recipients of these arancini balls, and we loved them so much, Kat was kind enough to share the recipe with us. Arancini are small rice balls filled with veggies and cheese, then coated in bread crumbs and fried. They are versatile, so add what you love!

SERVES 6 TO 8

Rice and Cheese Mixture

1 tablespoon olive oil

2 teaspoons butter

1 medium sweet onion (I like Vidalia), finely chopped

3 garlic cloves, minced

1½ cups Arborio rice

4 cups chicken stock

1 cup milk

¾ cup grated cheddar cheese

1 cup grated fontina cheese

1 large egg, at room temperature

1 teaspoon kosher salt

½ teaspoon freshly ground black pepper

1½ tablespoons finely chopped fresh parsley

Breading and Frying

3 quarts vegetable oil, for frying

¾ cup all-purpose flour

1 teaspoon kosher salt

½ teaspoon freshly ground black pepper

3 large eggs, at room temperature

2 tablespoons milk

3 cups panko bread crumbs

1 tablespoon Italian seasoning

Marinara sauce or Cherry Tomato Red Sauce (page 177), for serving

1 Preheat the oven to 350°F.

2 **MAKE THE RICE AND CHEESE MIXTURE:** In a Dutch oven, heat the olive oil and butter together over medium heat until combined and shimmering, about 2 minutes. Add the onion and cook until soft, 5 to 7 minutes. Add the garlic and cook for another 2 minutes. Add the rice and stir to toast for 1 minute. Add ½ cup of the stock and cook, stirring, until the liquid has been absorbed, 3 to 4 minutes. Add the milk and the remaining 3½ cups stock and bring to a simmer. Cover the Dutch oven tightly and transfer to the oven. Bake until all the liquid has been absorbed, 35 to 40 minutes. Remove from the oven and gently stir to loosen the rice from the pot. Let cool for 10 minutes with the lid off.

3 Transfer the rice to a large bowl and stir in the cheddar, fontina, egg, salt, pepper, and parsley. Spread the mixture out evenly in a large casserole dish, cover loosely, and cool in the refrigerator for at least 5 hours or up to overnight.

Recipe Continues

Me and Kat

4   **BREAD AND FRY THE ARANCINI:** Pour the oil into a large Dutch oven (it should come about 2 inches up the sides). Clip a deep-fry thermometer to its side and heat the oil over medium-high heat to 350°F.

5   Take the rice mixture out of the refrigerator. Using your hands, form the mixture into 2-tablespoon balls and set aside on a large baking sheet.

6   Set up a breading station using three shallow pans or bowls. In the first bowl, stir together the flour, salt, and pepper. In the second bowl, whisk together the eggs and milk until combined. In the third bowl, stir together the panko and Italian seasoning.

7   Roll the rice balls in the flour to coat, then the egg, then in the panko.

8   Fry the arancini in batches, turning them often to evenly cook, until golden brown, 3 to 4 minutes. Make sure you bring the oil back up to 350°F between batches.

9   Serve with your favorite marinara sauce.

TRISHA's TIPS

To add meat to these balls, cook ¼ pound lean ground beef until browned, and put about 1 teaspoon in the center of these rice balls as you roll them.

If you can't find fontina cheese, substitute mozzarella instead.

Arborio rice is the short-grained Italian rice used to make risotto; the rounded grains are firmer and creamier than other varieties due to their high starch content. Risotto requires a lot of stirring on the cooktop, time, and patience to keep it from sticking together. In the arancini, the Arborio rice helps the mixture hold together, so it can be rolled into balls and baked. The rice comes out sticky and lumped together, which is fine for this recipe.

TWICE-BAKED MAPLE BACON SWEET POTATOES

My love of all kinds of potatoes seems to be a running theme here! Beth and I grew up with the two greatest home cooks on the planet, our mom and dad. Our fondness for potatoes came from them, and they always made some form of potato skin or twice-baked potato. Beth and I took that idea and gave it our own twist by coming up with a savory twice-baked sweet potato skin with a hint of sweet maple syrup. When I make these delicious potatoes for Garth, I leave the hot sauce out of the mixture, then add it to my own potato. Yep, he's my cowboy, but he's a self-proclaimed spice wimp!

SERVES 4 TO 8

4 medium sweet potatoes

4 slices bacon

3 green onions, chopped

2 tablespoons pure maple syrup

1 teaspoon hot sauce (I like Tabasco)

5 ounces smoked cheddar cheese, shredded (about 1¼ cups)

Kosher salt and freshly ground black pepper

Sour cream, for serving

1 Preheat the oven to 400°F. Wash the sweet potatoes well and pierce the skin of each 3 or 4 times with a fork. Microwave on high for 10 minutes. Using a towel to hold them, prick with the tip of a knife to make sure it goes in easily. If there is resistance, microwave in 30-second increments until done, being careful not to overcook. The skin will puff up slightly when they are done and the knife will go in smoothly.

2 Meanwhile, using kitchen shears, cut the bacon into ½-inch pieces, dropping them into a medium skillet. Cook over medium heat until crisp and brown, about 7 minutes. Transfer to a paper towel–lined plate to drain. Reserve 1 tablespoon of the bacon fat.

3 Halve the sweet potatoes lengthwise. Using a teaspoon, carefully scoop most of the flesh out into a large bowl, leaving enough in the skin so that it holds its shape.

4 Add the bacon, reserved bacon fat, all but 2 tablespoons of the green onions, the maple syrup, hot sauce, and 1 cup of the cheese to the bowl with the sweet potato flesh. Stir together and season with salt and pepper to taste. Spoon the mixture into the sweet potato shells, placing them filled-side up on a baking sheet. Sprinkle the tops with the remaining cheese.

5 Bake until heated through and the cheese is melted, about 15 minutes. Top with the reserved 2 tablespoons green onions and a dollop of sour cream.

Be careful not to overcook the potatoes to make sure the outside shells remain firm. If you overcook them, the shells will fall apart when you try to scoop out the flesh.

FRENCH ONION SOUP

If French onion soup is offered on a restaurant's menu, I always order it. I love the sweet caramelized onions, the crispy bread, and all the melty cheese on top of the bowl. Yum! I think this is one of those soups that looks difficult to make, but the reality is, it's easy. The hardest part of the entire dish is being patient to slowly let the onions caramelize, but it's what makes the soup taste so delicious. I add Marsala wine, a Sicilian wine often used for cooking, in addition to the beef stock. This wine is especially good in helping create rich caramelized sauces, so it's perfect for this classic French onion soup.

SERVES 4

2 tablespoons extra-virgin olive oil

2 tablespoons butter

3 medium yellow onions, thinly sliced

4 sprigs thyme

1 bay leaf

2 garlic cloves, smashed and peeled

Kosher salt and freshly ground black pepper

½ cup sweet Marsala wine

6 cups beef stock

1 loaf Italian bread, cut into thick slices

8 ounces sliced whole-milk mozzarella cheese

1 cup shredded Gruyère cheese

Special Equipment
4 (2-cup) ovenproof bowls

1 In a large heavy-bottomed pot or Dutch oven, heat the olive oil and butter over medium heat until the butter melts, about 2 minutes. Add the onions, thyme, bay leaf, and garlic. Sprinkle the onion mixture with 1 teaspoon salt and ½ teaspoon pepper. Cook, stirring frequently, until the onions are soft and golden brown, 45 minutes.

2 Pour in the Marsala to deglaze the pot, stirring to scrape up any bits at the bottom. Add the stock and simmer until the onions are very soft and the soup has reduced slightly, about 35 minutes. Remove the thyme stems, bay leaf, and garlic cloves.

3 Preheat the broiler to high.

4 Put four slices of bread on a baking sheet. Toast the bread under the broiler until crispy and slightly golden brown, 1 to 2 minutes on each side.

5 Put four ovenproof serving bowls on the same baking sheet. Ladle the soup into the bowls (about 1½ cups per bowl). Top each bowl with a toasted slice of bread, then top the bread with a slice or two of mozzarella. Sprinkle ¼ cup of the Gruyère over each bowl.

6 Place the baking sheet of bowls under the broiler and broil until the cheese is melted and slightly browned, 1 to 2 minutes. Serve immediately.

Gruyère cheese has a creamy, nutty flavor that's perfect for this soup, but if you can't find it in your grocery store, use shredded Swiss cheese.

If you can't find Marsala wine or don't want to use it, substitute an extra ½ cup beef stock and 1 tablespoon sherry vinegar.

Pork & Beef

A lot of the recipes in this chapter were inspired by the amazing food I've enjoyed on my travels throughout the country while on tour, whether it was the perfect well-done steak in Portland, Oregon, or the discovery of the magic of BBQ burnt ends in Kansas City. If you're looking for fun ways to celebrate, try my party burger or giant meatballs. Yum!

GARTH'S TERIYAKI BOWL

When our girls were younger, they loved to eat at In the Raw, a sushi restaurant in downtown Tulsa. Garth and I are, to put it mildly, *not* fond of raw fish, so we had to find something on the menu to enjoy. We fell in love with their teriyaki rice bowl, and ordered it every time we went to In the Raw. When we moved back to Nashville, I created my own version of this awesome dish. Now that the girls are grown up, our family get-togethers are special occasions. I'm glad I can make this teriyaki bowl for all of us. Oh, and the sauce makes about 2 cups, but you might want to double the recipe. Garth could drink it with a straw!

SERVES 4

Marinated Chicken and Steak

2 tablespoons minced garlic

1 tablespoon cornstarch

2 teaspoons soy sauce

2 teaspoons rice vinegar

1 teaspoon kosher salt

½ teaspoon freshly ground black pepper

1 tablespoon olive oil

1 pound boneless, skinless chicken breast, cut into bite-size pieces

1 pound boneless sirloin steak, cut into bite-size pieces

Pineapple Teriyaki Sauce

4 teaspoons cornstarch

½ cup pineapple juice (reserved from pineapple below)

⅓ cup soy sauce

½ teaspoon ground ginger

¼ teaspoon garlic powder

¼ cup packed brown sugar

For the Bowls

1 tablespoon olive oil

2 green bell peppers, julienned

2 red bell peppers, julienned

2 yellow bell peppers, julienned

1 small onion, thinly sliced

Kosher salt

4 cups cooked long-grain white rice

2 (20-ounce) cans pineapple chunks in juice, drained, juices reserved (see Tips)

1 **MARINATE THE CHICKEN AND STEAK:** In a medium bowl, mix the garlic, cornstarch, soy sauce, vinegar, salt, pepper, and olive oil. Transfer half the marinade to a separate medium bowl. Add the chicken to one bowl and the beef to the other, and stir until the beef and chicken are covered completely. Set aside to marinate while you make the sauce.

2 **MAKE THE SAUCE:** In a small bowl, whisk together the cornstarch and 2 tablespoons water and set aside.

3 In a small stockpot, whisk together the pineapple juice, soy sauce, ginger, garlic powder, brown sugar, and ½ cup water and bring to a simmer over medium heat, about 4 minutes. Add the cornstarch mixture and whisk until the sauce thickens, about 3 minutes. Remove from the heat and set aside to cool.

4 Heat two medium skillets over medium heat for 1 to 2 minutes, then add the chicken to one skillet and the steak to the other and cook, stirring occasionally, until slightly browned, 4 to 6 minutes for the chicken and 5 to 7 minutes for the steak.

5 Meanwhile, in a medium saucepan, heat the olive oil over medium heat until shimmering, about 2 minutes. Add the bell peppers and onion with a pinch of salt and sauté until softened, about 5 minutes.

6 To assemble the bowls, divide the rice among individual serving bowls and top with the chicken and/or beef, sautéed vegetables, and pineapple chunks. Drizzle the teriyaki sauce over. Serve warm.

Substitute brown or yellow rice for the white rice for added flavor.

If you don't have rice vinegar, any vinegar will do.

Since you have olive oil in the marinade, you don't need to add oil to the skillets before cooking the steak and chicken.

When you drain the canned pineapple for the bowls, reserve ½ cup of the pineapple juice to use for the sauce.

TRISHA's TIPS

BBQ BURNT ENDS

I learned about this wonderful Midwest original on one of my tour stops in Kansas City, Missouri, several years ago. Normally, when you slow cook a brisket, the ends tend to burn a bit because they are thinner than the rest of the brisket. Sandwich makers and restauranteurs all over the country typically trim these bits off before serving brisket to their customers. Arthur Bryant's Barbeque restaurant in Kansas City started giving these burnt ends to customers while they waited in line for their sandwiches. Turns out, something that used to be tossed is one of the most flavorful bits of the brisket! To get this effect, I slow cook the whole brisket, dice it up, and cover it with sweet, smoky sauce, then broil it to get that caramelized effect. I should call it *brisket candy!*

SERVES 6 TO 8

Brisket

1½ tablespoons kosher salt

1½ teaspoons freshly ground black pepper

2 teaspoons smoked paprika

1 teaspoon cayenne pepper

1 teaspoon ground cumin

1 teaspoon granulated garlic

1 teaspoon dry mustard powder

5 pounds brisket, fat trimmed

BBQ Sauce

1 (6-ounce) can tomato paste

¼ cup packed dark brown sugar

2 tablespoons apple cider vinegar

½ teaspoon kosher salt

¼ teaspoon liquid smoke

¼ teaspoon cayenne pepper

¼ teaspoon granulated garlic

¼ teaspoon dry mustard powder

White bread or rolls, for serving

1 **MAKE THE BRISKET:** In a small bowl, combine the salt, pepper, paprika, cayenne, cumin, garlic, and dry mustard. Sprinkle the brisket on all sides with the spice rub. Place the brisket in a slow cooker, cover, and cook on high until tender, about 6 hours.

2 Remove the brisket from the slow cooker and set aside until cool enough to handle.

3 **MAKE THE BBQ SAUCE:** Pour the liquid from the slow cooker into a fat separator. Discard the fat and pour the cooking liquid into a stockpot. Stir in the tomato paste, brown sugar, vinegar, salt, liquid smoke, cayenne, granulated garlic, and dry mustard. Bring to a simmer over medium heat, then reduce the heat to medium-low. Simmer, stirring occasionally, until thickened, about 20 minutes.

4 Preheat the broiler to high.

5 Slice the brisket into 1-inch chunks. Remove and discard any large pieces of fat. Spread the brisket over a 9 x 13-inch baking pan and pour the BBQ sauce over the meat. Broil until crispy and slightly charred on the edges, about 5 minutes.

6 Serve warm, with bread or rolls.

If you don't have a fat separator, pour the liquid into a large measuring cup and allow the fat to rise to the top. Then, using a spoon, skim off the fat before adding the liquid to the stockpot.

BEEF MOUSSAKA

Are you wondering what a Greek dish is doing in a Georgia girl's food repertoire? I love all kinds of food, and I've learned that many meals from other cultures have similar counterparts around the world. For me, moussaka is lasagna's Greek cousin! This hearty meal uses eggplant for the "noodles," a sweet tomato sauce, and a creamy cheese sauce on top that rivals any lasagna I've ever tasted. Greece is on the list of places I want to visit in my life. For now, I'll settle for making the food myself and dreaming of the Aegean Sea!

SERVES 4

Eggplant and Meat Sauce

2 medium eggplants, cut into ¾-inch-thick rounds

⅓ cup plus 2 tablespoons olive oil

Kosher salt and freshly ground black pepper

1 pound lean ground beef

1 large onion, finely chopped

4 garlic cloves, minced

½ teaspoon red pepper flakes

½ teaspoon ground cinnamon

¼ teaspoon ground allspice

1 tablespoon tomato paste

½ cup dry white wine

1 (28-ounce) can crushed tomatoes, with their juices

1 tablespoon chopped fresh oregano

Cheese Sauce

4 tablespoons (½ stick) butter

⅓ cup all-purpose flour

1¾ cups whole milk

2 ounces crumbled goat cheese

1 cup grated Parmesan cheese

Kosher salt and freshly ground black pepper

2 large egg yolks

¼ cup chopped fresh parsley, for garnish

1 **MAKE THE EGGPLANT AND MEAT SAUCE:** Preheat the oven to 450°F.

2 Brush both sides of the eggplant slices with ⅓ cup of the olive oil and sprinkle with salt and black pepper. Arrange on a baking sheet and bake, turning once, until tender and golden brown on both sides, about 30 minutes. Reduce the oven temperature to 400°F. Line a rimmed baking sheet with aluminum foil.

3 In a large pot, heat the remaining 2 tablespoons oil over medium-high heat. Add the ground beef

and 1 teaspoon salt and cook until browned, about 6 minutes. Add the onion, garlic, and red pepper flakes and cook, stirring, until softened, about 6 minutes. Add the cinnamon, allspice, and tomato paste and cook, stirring, for 1 minute. Add the wine and boil until reduced by about half, about 3 minutes. Add the crushed tomatoes with their juices and the oregano and bring to a simmer. Simmer until slightly thickened and the flavors have blended, about 20 minutes. Season to taste with salt and black pepper.

4 **MEANWHILE, MAKE THE CHEESE SAUCE:** In a medium saucepan, melt the butter over medium heat, then whisk in the flour and cook for 1 minute. While whisking continuously, gradually add the milk. Bring to a simmer and whisk until thickened, 2 to 4 minutes. Remove from the heat and add the goat cheese and Parmesan, whisking until smooth. Season with salt and black pepper to taste. Whisk in the egg yolks.

5 Arrange half the eggplant rounds in a single layer over the bottom of an 8-inch square baking dish. Top with half the meat sauce. Layer the remaining eggplant rounds on top, followed by the remaining meat sauce. Top with an even layer of the cheese sauce. Place the baking dish on the prepared baking sheet and bake until the cheese sauce is bubbling and golden brown in spots, 20 to 30 minutes. Let stand for 20 minutes before serving.

6 Garnish with the parsley and serve warm.

CORNBREAD-CRUSTED FRIED PORK CHOPS

Growing up, fried pork chops were a "thing" in our family. As we all emerged from the '70s, like most families, we stopped frying so much, but occasionally I still love the deep-fried goodness of a pork chop, covered in my mama's white gravy. My Trisha twist is the cornbread breading, and a dash of hot sauce in my gravy! I think Mama would approve. Use your favorite cornbread recipe or a boxed version from the store, or try my Skillet Cheddar Cornbread (page 197).

SERVES 4

Pork Chops

4 (5- to 6-ounce) bone-in pork chops (I like center-cut)

Kosher salt and freshly ground black pepper

3 cups buttermilk

2 tablespoons hot sauce (I like Tabasco)

3 cups finely crumbled cornbread

1 quart vegetable oil, for frying

White Gravy

4 tablespoons (½ stick) butter

¼ cup all-purpose flour

2 cups whole milk

1 teaspoon hot sauce (I like Tabasco)

Kosher salt and freshly ground black pepper

2 tablespoons chopped fresh flat-leaf parsley, for garnish

1 MAKE THE PORK CHOPS: Sprinkle both sides of the pork chops liberally with salt and pepper. Combine the buttermilk and hot sauce in a large bowl. Put the pork chops in the buttermilk mixture, being sure that all four chops are submerged. Set aside to marinate for 30 minutes.

2 Preheat the oven to 300°F. Line a rimmed baking sheet with parchment paper and top with a wire rack.

3 Meanwhile, put the cornbread crumbs in a shallow dish.

4 Pour the oil into a large cast-iron skillet or other heavy-bottomed pan. Clip a deep-fry thermometer to its side and heat the oil over high heat to 350°F.

5 Using tongs, lift a pork chop out of the marinade by its top bone and allow any excess marinade to drip off. Lightly dredge the pork chop in the cornbread crumbs to coat both sides. Carefully lower the breaded chop into the hot oil. Repeat this process to bread a second chop. Fry the chops until crispy on one side, 3 to 4 minutes. Gently turn the pork chops and fry until golden brown on the second side, an additional 3 to 4 minutes. Transfer the crispy chops to the prepared rack. Sprinkle with salt and transfer to the oven to stay warm while you fry the remaining chops.

6 MAKE THE GRAVY: Reserve 2 tablespoons of the frying oil, then drain the skillet, being sure to remove any bits of fried cornbread left behind. Return the reserved oil to the skillet, add the butter, and heat over medium heat until the butter melts. Sprinkle in the flour and cook, whisking, until a smooth paste is formed, about 1 minute. While whisking continuously, pour in the milk, then cook, whisking occasionally, until the gravy thickens and coats the back of a spoon, 3 to 5 minutes. Stir in the hot sauce and season with salt and pepper to taste.

7 Transfer the crispy pork chops to a serving platter. Spoon the gravy over the chops and garnish with the parsley. Serve immediately.

HAVE-IT-YOUR-WAY STEAK

with Blue Cheese Compound Butter

This recipe was born because I love a well-done steak. I know! I can hear my dad Jack's voice in my head right now telling me how I'm ruining a good steak. He always ate his steaks medium-rare. I agree that well-done steaks can be shoe leather in the wrong hands. This seared and baked-in-the-oven method was inspired by the best well-done steak I ever tasted—it was in a restaurant in Portland, Oregon, when I was on tour in the '90s. I asked the chef how he got such an incredible, tender steak done all the way through without overcooking. He let me in on his oven-finishing secret! I've included temperatures and times for all levels of doneness so you can have it your way. No matter how you like your steak, you'll want to top it off with this creamy blue cheese compound butter.

SERVES 4

4 (10-ounce) beef tenderloin filets, 2 inches thick

½ cup (1 stick) butter, at room temperature, plus 1 tablespoon

3 ounces blue cheese crumbles

Kosher salt and freshly ground black pepper

1 tablespoon vegetable oil

1 Preheat the oven to 425°F.

2 Remove the filets from the refrigerator and let them come to room temperature for 30 minutes.

3 Meanwhile, in a food processor, combine the stick of butter, the blue cheese, ¾ teaspoon salt, and ¼ teaspoon pepper. Process until well blended and smooth. Transfer to a sheet of plastic wrap and roll into a cylinder about 2 inches in diameter. Wrap tightly and place in the freezer to chill.

4 Season both sides of the filets with salt and pepper. In a large skillet, heat the oil and remaining 1 tablespoon butter over high heat until the butter has melted and the skillet is very hot. Place the filets in the hot pan and sear for 2 minutes on the first side, then flip and sear on the second side for 2 minutes. Transfer the skillet (don't forget that it's hot—use oven mitts!) to the oven and bake to your desired doneness (see box).

5 Take the blue cheese butter out of the freezer and slice it into ¼-inch-thick rounds. Serve each filet topped with a butter round.

 TRISHA'S TIPS

Letting the filets come to room temperature allows for more even cooking and more accurate cooking times.

When selecting cuts of meat, plan for at least 8 ounces (uncooked) per person.

Doneness temperatures and oven time for steak

RARE: 120° to 125°F / 4 minutes

MEDIUM-RARE: 125° to 130°F / 5 to 6 minutes

MEDIUM: 135° to 140°F / 6 to 7 minutes

MEDIUM-WELL: 145° to 150°F / 8 to 9 minutes

WELL-DONE: 160°F and above / 10+ minutes

RED CHILI TAMALE PIE

My guitar player and good friend Johnny Garcia used to bring his mom's homemade tamales on the road every year and share them with me because he knew I loved them so much. They are a labor of love because they take time and patience. Patience is not my superpower, so I created my own version of a deconstructed tamale and made it easy on myself! This pie gives me all the flavors I love about a traditional tamale in a fraction of the time.

SERVES 6

3 tablespoons corn oil

½ pound ground beef

½ pound ground pork

1 medium red onion, finely chopped

1 garlic clove, minced

Kosher salt

2 tablespoons tomato paste

2 teaspoons chili powder

½ teaspoon ground cumin

1 (10-ounce) can red enchilada sauce

1 cup canned pinto beans, drained and rinsed

1 cup frozen corn kernels, thawed

¼ cup chopped fresh cilantro

1½ cups shredded pepper Jack cheese

2 cups self-rising buttermilk cornmeal mix (see Tip)

1½ to 2 cups buttermilk

¼ cup diced roasted red pepper

1 Preheat the oven to 400°F.

2 In a 10-inch cast-iron skillet, heat 1 tablespoon of the oil over medium-high heat. Add the beef, pork, onions, garlic, and 1 teaspoon salt and cook, stirring and breaking up any clumps with a wooden spoon, until the meat is browned and the onion is softened, about 6 minutes.

3 Add the tomato paste, chili powder, and cumin and cook, stirring, for about 1 minute. Stir in the enchilada sauce, beans, corn, and cilantro and season with salt. Bring to a simmer. Remove from the heat and sprinkle with the cheese.

4 Put the cornmeal mix in a large bowl. Stir in 1½ cups of the buttermilk and the remaining 2 tablespoons oil. The mixture should be thick but pourable, so add up to another ½ cup buttermilk if necessary.

5 Stir in the peppers. Pour the batter over the meat mixture in the skillet and spread it into an even layer. Bake until the meat is bubbling and the cornbread is golden brown, 20 to 25 minutes. Let the tamale pie cool for 10 minutes before serving.

If you don't have self-rising buttermilk cornmeal mix, make your own by mixing 1¾ cups finely ground cornmeal, 6 tablespoons all-purpose flour, 2 tablespoons baking powder, and ½ teaspoon kosher salt.

GIANT MEATBALLS IN MARINARA

My friend and neighbor, Kathy, is 100 percent Italian. I love her spirit, her sense of humor, and her strong sense of family. When she and her husband, Matt, and her mom, Stephania, come to my house for dinner, I never cook Italian food. I leave it to the professionals! I did convince Kathy to be on my cooking show, and we made our favorite Italian dishes together. These meatballs were a hit. If Kat loves them, they're *"perfetto!"* These giant meatballs make an impressive presentation, but you can make regular-size meatballs if you prefer.

SERVES 4

Meatballs

Extra-virgin olive oil, for brushing

¼ cup roughly chopped fresh flat-leaf parsley

3 garlic cloves, smashed and peeled

1 medium carrot, cut into chunks

1 celery stalk, cut into chunks

1 small onion, cut into chunks

2 large eggs, beaten

¼ cup milk

Kosher salt and freshly ground black pepper

½ cup fine dried bread crumbs

½ cup grated Parmesan cheese

1 pound ground beef

1 pound ground pork

Marinara

¼ cup extra-virgin olive oil

1 medium onion, chopped

4 garlic cloves, sliced

¼ teaspoon red pepper flakes

½ teaspoon dried oregano

2 (28-ounce) can whole tomatoes

Kosher salt

1 cup grated Parmesan cheese, plus more for serving

½ cup loosely packed fresh basil leaves, chopped

1 **MAKE THE MEATBALLS:** Preheat the oven to 425°F. Line a rimmed baking sheet with parchment paper and brush the parchment with olive oil.

2 In a food processor, combine the parsley, garlic, carrot, celery, and onion and pulse to make an almost-smooth paste. Transfer to a large bowl.

3 In a small bowl, whisk together the eggs and milk, then add to the vegetable paste. Sprinkle with salt and pepper. Add the bread crumbs, Parmesan, ground beef, and ground pork. Mix well using your hands. Form the meat mixture into 6 large meatballs, about 3 inches in diameter, and place on the prepared baking sheet. Make sure the meatballs aren't touching. Bake until the meatballs are just cooked through, about 40 minutes.

4 **MEANWHILE, MAKE THE MARINARA SAUCE:** Heat a large Dutch oven over medium heat. Add the olive oil and onion and cook until softened, about 5 minutes. Add the garlic and red pepper flakes and cook for 1 minute. Add the oregano, tomatoes, 1 teaspoon salt, and 1 cup water and smash the tomatoes with the back of a wooden spoon to break them up. Reduce the heat to maintain a simmer and cook until slightly thickened, about 20 minutes.

5 Add the meatballs to the marinara sauce, and toss to combine. Top with the Parmesan and sprinkle with the basil to serve.

TRISHA's TIP

For regular-size meatballs, use about 2 tablespoons of the meat mixture per meatball. Bake for 15 to 20 minutes.

CHILI MAC

Everyone has their own version of chili mac and cheese. Traditionally, it's a cooked macaroni with some cheese and some cooked ground beef and tomatoes. This dish came out of my wanting just MORE of everything, so I make a complete recipe of macaroni and cheese, a complete chili recipe, and then combine the two together. The result is a super cheesy, meaty, true chili mac and cheese. The addition of cream cheese takes this comfort food to the next level. I hope you love it as much as I do! Garth loves to eat this chili mac almost like dip, using big corn chip scoops or tortilla chip scoops.

SERVES 8

Kosher salt

16 ounces elbow macaroni

2 tablespoons vegetable oil

1 medium red onion, chopped

1 red bell pepper, chopped

4 garlic cloves, minced

1 pound lean ground beef

Freshly ground black pepper

1 tablespoon chili powder

1 tablespoon ground cumin

2 teaspoons paprika

1 teaspoon dried oregano

2 (15-ounce) cans kidney beans, undrained

2 (14.5-ounce) cans diced tomatoes, with their juices

¼ cup tomato paste

4 tablespoons (½ stick) butter

¼ cup all-purpose flour

4 cups milk

1 (8-ounce) package cream cheese, at room temperature

8 ounces sharp cheddar cheese, grated, plus more for serving

2 teaspoons Dijon mustard

2 teaspoons Worcestershire sauce

4 green onions, chopped

Corn chips or tortilla chip scoops, for serving

1 Bring a large pot of water to a boil. Add a generous pinch of salt and then the macaroni. Cook to al dente according to the package directions. Drain and set aside.

2 In a medium pot, heat the oil over medium heat. Add the red onion, cover, and cook until soft, 2 to 4 minutes. Add the bell pepper and cook for 2 to 5 minutes more. Add the garlic and cook for 1 minute more.

3 Add the ground beef and sprinkle with salt and black pepper. Cook, stirring to break up the beef into small pieces, until browned, 7 to 8 minutes. Add the chili powder, cumin, paprika, and oregano and cook until the spices are fragrant, about 2 minutes. Add the beans and their liquid, the tomatoes and their juices, and the tomato paste; stir to combine. Simmer for 5 to 10 minutes.

4 In a separate large saucepot, melt the butter over low heat. Add the flour and cook, whisking, for 1 minute. Whisk in the milk, raise the heat to high, and bring the mixture to a boil. Reduce the heat to medium and continue to cook, whisking, until thickened, 5 to 6 minutes. Remove from the heat and whisk in the cream cheese, cheddar, mustard, and Worcestershire. Season with salt and black pepper to taste.

5 Pour the pasta into the cheese sauce and stir to combine.

6 Mix the chili into the macaroni and cheese. Transfer to a serving bowl and top with additional cheddar and the green onions. Serve with corn chips.

TRISHA'S TIPS

The cream cheese doesn't have to be at room temperature before it's added to the cheese sauce, but it does blend together more quickly and easily if it is. I recommend taking your cream cheese block out of the fridge and letting it come to room temperature while you're cooking your pasta and chili. Chop it into chunks before adding it to the sauce.

If the ground beef releases a lot of fat as you're browning it, drain it in a colander, then return it to the pot before adding the spices and finishing up the chili.

THE PARTY BURGER

Yes, you could make regular old burgers, but why would you when you can make a party burger? This is a showstopper for sure! The trickiest part of the whole process is flipping this big burger in the skillet. I recommend two spatulas and a lot of patience! Then when it's time to flip . . . go for it, no hesitation. For the enormous bun, I halve a boule (pronounced *bool*) which is just French bread in the shape of a ball. It's the perfect shape and size for this larger-than-life burger. I whisk together all the condiments that I normally put on a burger, and top it with all the traditional burger fixins for this monster of a meal! After everyone's done *ooh*ing and *ahh*ing over this burger, slice it into sections like you would a pizza, and serve.

◆

SERVES 4 TO 6

2 tablespoons ketchup

2 tablespoons mayonnaise

2 tablespoons mustard

½ teaspoon freshly ground black pepper

2 pounds 80% lean ground sirloin

Kosher salt

1 tablespoon vegetable oil

6 or 7 slices American cheese

1 small boule (round bread loaf), sliced in half horizontally

3 green-leaf lettuce leaves

1 plum tomato, sliced

8 dill pickle slices

1   In a small bowl, whisk together the ketchup, mayonnaise, mustard, and pepper. Set aside.

2   Find a bowl or pan that is just bigger than your loaf of bread and place on a piece of parchment paper. Trace around the bowl with a pen and flip the parchment over. Roll the ground sirloin into a big ball, then place it on the parchment and press it into a patty, using the traced circle as a guide. Sprinkle both sides with 1 teaspoon salt.

3   Heat a cast-iron skillet or griddle over medium-high heat. Once hot, add the oil and heat until shimmering, about 1 minute. Add the patty to the pan and press down firmly with a spatula. This monster burger patty will be about 1½ inches thick. Cook until the edges are crispy and deeply golden brown, 3 to 4 minutes per side. Fan the cheese over the burger and invert a metal bowl or baking sheet over the skillet. Cook until the cheese melts and gets crispy on the edges touching the pan, about 2 minutes more.

4   Spread the sauce on the cut sides of the boule. Place the burger on the bottom half of the boule. Top with the lettuce, tomato, pickles, and a sprinkle of salt. Set the top of the boule on top and slice into quarters or sixths to serve.

SMOKED HAM CARBONARA

I love carbonara, an Italian pasta dish traditionally made with eggs and some kind of cured pork, usually pancetta. Carbonara comes from Rome, but I put my Georgia spin on this classic dish by using smoked country ham. Don't be put off by the raw eggs in this dish. The eggs essentially get cooked by tossing them with the hot pasta. They don't scramble, but they cook just enough to thicken into a creamy sauce. I make this carbonara with leftover ham from Easter or Christmas dinner.

SERVES 4 TO 6

Kosher salt

2 tablespoons olive oil

1 small sweet onion (I like Vidalia), chopped

2 garlic cloves, grated

16 ounces spaghetti

8 to 10 ounces smoked ham, diced small

2 cups freshly grated Parmesan cheese

1 cup heavy cream

4 large eggs

Freshly ground black pepper

1 Bring a large pot of salted water to a boil.

2 Meanwhile, in a medium saucepan, heat the olive oil over medium-low heat. Add the onion and sauté, stirring occasionally, until soft and starting to caramelize, about 20 minutes. Add the garlic and cook until softened, 3 to 5 minutes.

3 Meanwhile, cook the spaghetti in the boiling water according to the package directions, about 8 minutes.

4 Add the ham to the pan with the onion and garlic and cook until just warmed through, about 2 minutes.

5 In a medium bowl, whisk together the Parmesan, cream, eggs, 1½ teaspoons salt, and a pinch of pepper.

6 Drain the pasta and transfer to the saucepan with the onion mixture and toss well. Immediately stir in the egg-cheese mixture until well combined. Serve immediately.

TRISHA's TIP

Make the spaghetti after caramelizing the onions so the pasta doesn't sit and get cool. Mixing in the egg-cheese mixture with the hot pasta is the key to the creamy sauce.

SAUSAGE & BUTTERBEAN SKILLET DINNER

Beth and I grew up with a big garden. One of our summer chores was to help shell beans and peas. Butterbeans were always a huge crop for us, and our thumbs got sore from shelling all of them, but we didn't mind because we loved the taste of fresh-cooked garden vegetables so much! Our mom most often simply boiled them in a little salted water and finished them with a pat of butter, but we've found all sorts of ways to use these dense beans in other dishes. Combining them with spicy andouille sausage and serving over rice is perfection. I love any meal cooked in a cast-iron skillet!

SERVES 4

1 bunch rainbow chard (about 1 pound)

14 to 16 ounces smoked sausage (I like andouille)

2 tablespoons vegetable oil

1 sweet onion (I like Vidalia), halved and thinly sliced

Kosher salt and freshly ground black pepper

²⁄₃ cup chicken stock

8 ounces frozen butterbeans (1½ cups), thawed

1 tablespoon sherry vinegar

3½ cups warm cooked rice

1 Remove the stems from the chard and tear the leaves into 2-inch pieces. Slice the sausage at an angle into ½-inch-thick rounds.

2 In a large cast-iron skillet, heat 1 tablespoon of the oil over medium-high heat until it shimmers. Add the sausage, cut-side down, and sear for 2 to 3 minutes. Turn it over and sear for another 2 minutes. Transfer the sausage to a plate and set aside.

3 Add the remaining 1 tablespoon oil to the skillet. Add the onion with a pinch each of salt and pepper and cook for 7 to 8 minutes, until softened and browned.

4 Add the stock, butterbeans, half the chard, and another pinch of salt. Cover and simmer for 3 minutes. Carefully lift the lid to avoid the steam, stir, and add the remaining chard. Cover and cook for another 3 minutes.

5 Add the sausage in an even layer, tucked between the chard and onion. Simmer to warm the sausage through, about 2 minutes. Stir in the vinegar and serve over warm rice.

 TRISHA'S TIPS

If you can't find rainbow chard at your local grocery store, regular chard is fine! You can also substitute Tuscan kale and cook it just as you would the chard, or you can add 8 ounces fresh spinach after cooking the butterbeans for 6 minutes and cook until the spinach is wilted before returning the sausage to the skillet. The greens are interchangeable!

I use spicy andouille sausage for this skillet dinner, but kielbasa works well, too.

Chicken, Turkey & Fish

There's so much more to life than just plain old grilled chicken, turkey slices, and baked fish! You've got so many flavor choices here, from sweet cornflake-crusted catfish planks to the best turkey meatloaf you ever tasted. I've even spun classic chicken potpie into a burger. Trust me, you'll want to sample every single recipe in this chapter!

CHICKEN POTPIE BURGERS

This burger just might become one of your family favorites. It combines all the savory vegetable flavors of my mama's classic chicken potpie and puts it on a bun. The sweet English pea gravy takes this dish home. It's truly incredible to bite into this burger and taste all the flavors of a perfect potpie. It's a comfort burger!

MAKES 4 BURGERS

4 tablespoons (½ stick) butter

2 small celery stalks, finely chopped

1 small carrot, grated

1 medium shallot, finely chopped

¼ teaspoon powdered chicken bouillon

¼ teaspoon celery seeds

Kosher salt

2 tablespoons all-purpose flour

¼ teaspoon garlic powder

1 cup plus 2 tablespoons milk

⅓ cup frozen peas

Freshly ground black pepper

¼ cup panko bread crumbs

1 pound ground chicken

Nonstick cooking spray

4 hamburger buns, lightly toasted

1 In a cast-iron skillet, melt 2 tablespoons of the butter over medium heat. Add the celery, carrot, shallot, bouillon, celery seeds, and ¼ teaspoon salt and cook, stirring occasionally, until softened, about 7 minutes. Transfer to a large bowl and let cool to room temperature.

2 Meanwhile, in a small saucepan, melt the remaining 2 tablespoons butter over medium heat. Add the flour and garlic powder and cook, whisking, for about 1 minute. Gradually add 1 cup of the milk and bring the mixture to a simmer, whisking continuously. Continue to simmer, whisking, until thickened, about 2 minutes. Add the peas, ½ teaspoon salt, and a generous amount of pepper. Remove from the heat and cover to keep warm.

3 Mix the panko into the cooked vegetables, then stir in the remaining 2 tablespoons milk and let stand for 5 minutes. Add the ground chicken, 1 teaspoon salt, and a dash of pepper.

4 Form the chicken mixture into four ¾-inch-thick patties. Spray the skillet and one side of the patties with nonstick spray. Heat the skillet over medium-high heat, then place the patties in the skillet, sprayed-side down, and spray the tops of the patties. Reduce the heat to medium, then cover and cook for 2 minutes. Flip the patties and cook, uncovered, until they are cooked all the way through and the centers are firm, about 2 minutes more.

5 Serve on the buns, topped with the pea gravy, with extra gravy on the side.

COMPANY CHICKEN

In our house, when somebody was coming for a visit, we'd be told to straighten up the living room because "company's coming!" If we were having guests who were staying for supper, well then the dish needed to be *extra* special. When Beth's family moved to South Georgia, her neighbor Venita served this dish and it became a regular addition to our family recipe box. It's definitely special enough for company, or "comp'ny," as my dad would say!

SERVES 6

6 boneless, skinless chicken breasts

4 (.6-ounce) packets Italian dressing mix

2 tablespoons vegetable oil

2 tablespoons butter

1 pound white mushrooms, sliced

Kosher salt

¾ cup dry white wine

6 ounces (¾ of an 8-ounce package) cream cheese, at room temperature

1 (10¾-ounce) can cream of mushroom soup

2 tablespoons chopped fresh flat-leaf parsley, for garnish

1 Preheat the oven to 350°F.

2 Coat the chicken breasts in the dressing mix.

3 In a large nonstick skillet, heat the oil over medium-high heat until very hot. Add the chicken and cook until well browned, about 4 minutes. Turn the chicken, add the butter to the pan, and cook until the chicken is just golden brown, about 3 minutes more. Transfer the chicken to a large baking dish.

4 Add the mushrooms and a pinch of salt to the skillet and cook, stirring occasionally, until golden brown, about 10 minutes. Spoon the mushrooms on top of the chicken.

5 Pour the wine into the hot skillet and bring to a simmer, stirring to scrape up any browned bits from the pan. Stir in the cream cheese and the mushroom soup until well combined and heated through. Pour the sauce over the chicken and mushrooms.

6 Bake, uncovered, until the chicken is cooked through, 30 minutes. Sprinkle with the parsley and serve warm.

TRISHA'S TIP

Room-temperature cream cheese melts into the sauce much faster. Take the cream cheese out of your fridge and leave it on your countertop for 1 hour to soften. If you don't have an hour to wait, you can cut the cream cheese into cubes and set them out on your countertop. They will soften in about 10 minutes.

Comp'ny Chicken

TURKEY MEATLOAF

I grew up on Mama's basic four-ingredient ground beef meatloaf, and I absolutely love it, but meatloaf is one of those dishes that I will order on a menu and always enjoy, no matter how it may differ from what I'm used to. This turkey meatloaf is a delicious departure from the usual fare. Pulsing the rich, dark-meat ground turkey in a food processor gives this meatloaf an almost pâté texture. The sweet, ketchup-based sauce on top is adapted from a barbecue glaze we use every Fourth of July on pork ribs. It works amazingly well on this bacon-topped turkey goodness. If meatloaf can be elegant, this is it!

SERVES 6

Barbecue Glaze

1 (14-ounce) bottle ketchup

1 (12-ounce) bottle chili sauce

½ cup packed brown sugar

1 teaspoon dry mustard powder

Meatloaf

3 teaspoons olive oil

2 small onions, finely chopped

3 tablespoons chopped fresh parsley

1 carrot, finely chopped

1½ pounds ground dark meat turkey

¾ cup seasoned bread crumbs

¼ cup ketchup

1 large egg, whisked

Kosher salt and freshly ground black pepper

6 slices bacon

1   Preheat the oven to 350°F.

2   **MAKE THE GLAZE:** In a large saucepan, stir together the ketchup, chili sauce, brown sugar, dry mustard, and ⅓ cup water. Bring to a boil, stirring to dissolve the sugar. Remove from the heat and set aside.

3   **MAKE THE MEATLOAF:** In a small skillet, heat 2 teaspoons of the oil over medium-low heat until shimmering, about 2 minutes. Add the onions and cook until softened and browned, about 10 minutes. Add the parsley and cook for 1 to 2 minutes. Transfer the mixture to a medium bowl and set aside to cool.

4   Add the remaining 1 teaspoon oil to the skillet. Add the carrot and cook over medium heat until softened, about 5 minutes. Remove from the heat.

5   In a food processor, combine the ground turkey, bread crumbs, ketchup, egg, onion mixture, 1 teaspoon salt, and a pinch of pepper and pulse until fully combined. Transfer to a large bowl and stir in the carrots to combine.

6   Form the turkey mixture into a loaf and transfer to a casserole dish or baking sheet. Using a pastry brush, spread the BBQ glaze over the top. Drape the bacon over the loaf in a crisscross pattern, tucking the ends underneath. Brush more glaze over the bacon layer.

7   Bake until the meatloaf is firm and cooked through, 55 to 60 minutes. Let rest for 5 minutes before slicing and serving.

I don't puree the carrots with the rest of the mixture to give some bright bits of color when you slice into the finished product.

The dark meat ground turkey gives this meatloaf its rich taste.

HOT CHICKEN CHILI

I talk a lot about how my husband doesn't "DO" spicy. Well, this might be the exception to his rule. He loves this chicken chili so much that he tolerates the heat that makes this chili true to its Nashville hot chicken roots. While the chili isn't super spicy, it's easily adjusted for those of us who like more heat. Just add some extra spiced oil to your own bowl like I do! This chili goes great served over corn chips, or, if your spice meter goes all the way to the top, try it with my Hot Honey Cornbread (page 192).

SERVES 4 TO 6

1 cup vegetable oil

3 tablespoons cayenne pepper

2 tablespoons light brown sugar

1 teaspoon paprika

1 teaspoon garlic powder

2 teaspoons kosher salt

2 carrots, finely diced

1 medium yellow onion, finely diced

2 pounds ground chicken

2 (15.5-ounce) cans cannellini beans, drained and rinsed

1 (14-ounce) can diced tomatoes, with their juices

2 teaspoons hot sauce (I like Tabasco)

1 cup chicken stock

1 cup sour cream, for serving

¼ cup chopped bread-and-butter pickles, for garnish

1   In a small saucepan, stir together the oil, cayenne, brown sugar, paprika, garlic powder, and 1 teaspoon of the salt. Cook over low heat until the spices infuse the oil, 2 to 3 minutes.

2   Heat a large Dutch oven or heavy-bottomed pan over medium heat. Spoon ¼ cup of the spiced oil into the pan. Add the carrots and onion and cook until the vegetables soften and start to brown, 6 to 8 minutes. Add the ground chicken and the remaining 1 teaspoon salt and cook, breaking up the chicken with a wooden spoon, until browned, 7 to 8 minutes.

3   Add the beans, tomatoes with their juices, hot sauce, and 2 tablespoons more spiced oil. Stir together and bring to a boil. Add the stock and return to a boil, then reduce the heat to maintain a simmer, cover with the lid slightly ajar to allow steam to escape, and cook, stirring occasionally, until the chili is thickened, 15 to 20 minutes.

4   Ladle the chili into bowls. Top each bowl with a dollop of sour cream, a sprinkle of chopped pickles, and a drizzle of the remaining spicy oil.

CREAMY CHICKEN NOODLE SOUP

Home-cooked chicken soup is a like a warm hug on those days when the weather is rainy and cool, or when you're feeling a little *under* the weather. Most of my chicken soup recipes have a thinner broth, which is perfect when that's your preference. But if you're in the mood for something a little heartier, this creamy soup has a real stick-to-your ribs vibe. Take my suggestion and pick up a rotisserie chicken on your way home to get this comfort meal on the table faster. This creamy soup makes me look forward to soup weather!

SERVES 5

6 tablespoons (¾ stick) butter

1 medium yellow onion, diced

3 medium carrots, chopped

3 celery stalks, chopped

Kosher salt and freshly ground black pepper

2 garlic cloves, peeled

4 cups chicken stock

1 bay leaf

2 sprigs fresh thyme

2 cups medium egg noodles

2 tablespoons all-purpose flour

2¼ cups whole milk

⅓ cup heavy cream

1 rotisserie chicken, meat shredded (about 5 cups meat; save the bones to make stock for another time)

3 tablespoons chopped fresh parsley

1 In a large heavy-bottomed pot, melt 2 tablespoons of the butter over medium-high heat. Once the butter begins to foam, add the onion, carrots, celery, a big pinch of salt, and a pinch of pepper. Sauté until the vegetables begin to get tender, about 5 minutes. Grate in the garlic and cook for another minute.

2 Add the stock, bay leaf, and thyme and bring to a simmer. Gently cook the vegetables, stirring occasionally, until tender, about 10 minutes.

3 Remove the bay leaf and thyme from the soup and add the noodles. Cook for about 5 minutes, pressing down occasionally to make sure the noodles are submerged.

4 In a medium saucepan, melt the remaining 4 tablespoons (½ stick) butter over medium heat. As soon as the butter is melted, scatter in the flour and whisk to incorporate with the butter. Whisk until the roux smells a little toasted, about 2 minutes. Slowly whisk in the milk, blending so there are no lumps. Add the cream and bring to a simmer over medium heat, stirring continuously, then cook until the mixture has thickened, 3 to 5 minutes. Remove from the heat.

5 Add the cream mixture, chicken, and parsley to the soup, stirring for a minute to warm the chicken through but not allowing the soup to boil. Taste for seasoning and add salt and pepper if needed.

DRY-BRINED GRILLED CHICKEN

Grilled chicken often gets a bad rap. It can certainly be boring, but this dry brine really spices things up! I use dark meat chicken for this dish. The dark drumsticks and thighs of the chicken are richer and fattier so they start your dish off a step ahead. The dry-brining method is a great way to impart a lot of flavor to your chicken by seasoning it the night before, but keeping it dry so you still get a crispy skin.

SERVES 4

1 tablespoon plus 1 teaspoon kosher salt

2 teaspoons brown sugar

½ teaspoon freshly ground black pepper

½ teaspoon dried thyme

½ teaspoon smoked paprika

¼ teaspoon garlic powder

¼ teaspoon onion powder

4 bone-in, skin-on chicken thighs

4 bone-in, skin-on drumsticks

Your favorite sauce, Peach Mustard Barbecue Sauce (page 210), or Trisha's Sweet & Smoky Hot Sauce (page 208), for serving

1 In a small bowl, combine the salt, sugar, pepper, thyme, paprika, garlic powder, and onion powder.

2 Pat the chicken dry with a paper towel and place in a medium bowl. Season the meat all over with the spice mixture, cover, and refrigerate overnight.

3 The next day, place the chicken skin-side up on a plate and let come to room temperature for 30 minutes.

4 Heat a grill to 400°F or high heat. Add the chicken skin-side down and reduce the heat to medium-high. Cover the grill and cook, without moving the chicken around, for 10 minutes, then flip the chicken and cook until the temperature of the meat reaches 165°F, taken close to but not touching the bone, 7 to 9 minutes.

5 Remove the chicken from the grill and let rest for 10 minutes before serving. Enjoy with your favorite sauce.

Trisha's Tips

If you are using a charcoal grill, heat with your coals to one side of the grill and cook your chicken on the side without the coals.

Taking the chicken's temperature with a meat thermometer inserted close to the bone but not touching it will give you the most accurate temperature measurement.

LOBSTER MAC & CHEESE

When Garth played his one-man show in Las Vegas for four years, our girls were in high school. If they didn't have soccer games, they would sometimes head to Vegas with us for those fun-filled music weekends, and their big excitement was room service! I was so proud of Taylor, August, and Allie for trying new things. One of their favorite dishes to order from the fantastic Wynn kitchen was lobster mac and cheese. I have to admit, I was in my forties and I had never even tried it before then! Lobster definitely takes mac and cheese to new heights, and the pancetta gives it a salty, crispy vibe that's really yummy. I'm grateful the girls turned me on to such a wonderful way to amp up comfort food!

SERVES 6 TO 8

Kosher salt

16 ounces large elbow macaroni

4 tablespoons butter, plus more for greasing

5 (4-ounce) cold-water lobster tails, thawed in the fridge overnight if frozen

1 lemon, quartered

8 ounces Colby Jack cheese, grated

8 ounces Gruyère cheese, grated

¾ cup grated Parmesan cheese

8 ounces pancetta, diced

¼ cup all-purpose flour

3 cups milk

¼ teaspoon freshly ground black pepper

Pinch of cayenne pepper

Topping

2 tablespoons butter

½ cup panko bread crumbs

¼ teaspoon Old Bay seasoning

1 Preheat the oven to 425°F, with a rack in the center.

2 In a large stockpot, bring 4 quarts water to a boil and season with 3 tablespoons salt. Cook the pasta to al dente according to the package directions. Drain the pasta fully and return it to the pot. Toss it with 2 tablespoons of the butter and set aside.

3 Place the lobster tails on a damp dish towel on the countertop to keep them from sliding, and use kitchen shears to cut the top of each tail open lengthwise, from the open end to the last segment. Place the lobsters in a 9 x 13-inch baking dish with ½ cup water. Squeeze the lemon quarters over the lobster and tuck the quarters into the water among the tails.

4 Place the lobsters in the center of the oven and roast for 10 minutes. (This will not fully cook the lobster; it will finish cooking when baked in the mac and cheese.) Transfer the lobster tails to a plate until cool enough to touch. Reduce the oven temperature to 350°F.

5 Crack the lobster tails and remove the meat from the shells. Discard the shells and roughly chop the meat into ½-inch pieces; set aside. Rinse out the casserole dish, grease with butter, and set aside.

6 In a medium bowl, stir together the Colby Jack, Gruyère, and ½ cup of the Parmesan and set aside.

7 Heat a high-sided 2- to 4-quart saucepan over medium-high heat. Add the pancetta and cook for 6 minutes, until it starts to crisp. Remove with a slotted spoon, leaving the fat in the pan.

8 Toss the cooked pancetta with the pasta.

9 In the saucepan with the reserved fat, melt the remaining 2 tablespoons butter into the pancetta fat over medium heat, then shake in the flour, whisking until smooth to make a roux. Cook until the roux turns a pale brown, about 2 minutes.

Recipe Continues

10 Slowly whisk in 1 cup of the milk to avoid lumps, then whisk in 1 cup more milk. Cook, stirring continuously, until the sauce thickens slightly, about 5 minutes. Add ½ teaspoon salt, the black pepper, and the cayenne pepper and whisk to combine. Reduce the heat to low and stir in the cheeses in two parts until melted and creamy. Whisk in the remaining 1 cup milk until fully combined.

11 Pour the cheese sauce over the pasta and stir to combine. Once the pasta is fully coated, stir in the lobster meat and pour the mixture into the prepared casserole dish. Sprinkle the remaining ¼ cup Parmesan on top of the mixture.

12 MAKE THE TOPPING: In a small skillet, melt the butter over medium heat. Stir in the panko and Old Bay and toast for 2 to 3 minutes.

13 Sprinkle the crumb topping over the casserole and bake for 30 to 35 minutes, until bubbling and lightly toasted on top. Let the casserole cool for 15 minutes before serving.

Pancetta is basically Italian bacon. You can substitute bacon if you can't find pancetta.

SHRIMP CREOLE

During Mama's years teaching third grade, a teacher friend, Wendy, shared her family's recipe for this flavorful soup. When Beth got married (thirty-five years ago!), she tried it out for a special occasion meal. Recently, her husband John asked if she still had the recipe, and she made it for the family. Their youngest, Bret, loved it and wondered where it had been all his life! I'm with ya, Bret! Boiling the shrimp shells in the broth is really the flavor magic in this dish.

◆

SERVES 4

1 pound medium shrimp (about 40), peeled and deveined (save the shells)

2 cups chicken stock

6 tablespoons (¾ stick) butter, cubed

Kosher salt

1 large yellow onion, finely chopped (about 1½ cups)

1 large green bell pepper, finely chopped (about 1 cup)

2 celery stalks, finely diced

Pinch of freshly ground black pepper

¼ cup tomato paste

2 garlic cloves, minced

2 tablespoons dry sherry

1 bay leaf

1 tablespoon Worcestershire sauce

1 teaspoon sugar

2 to 4 shakes Tabasco sauce, plus more as desired

4 cups warm cooked rice, for serving

Leaves from 1 bunch flat-leaf parsley, chopped, for garnish

1 In a medium saucepan, combine the shrimp shells and stock, bring to a boil, then reduce the heat to medium and cook for 5 minutes. Strain the stock, discarding the shrimp shells, and set aside.

2 In a large sauté pan, melt the butter over medium-high heat. Add the shrimp in an even layer, sprinkle lightly with salt, and cook on both sides until the shrimp turn light pink but are still tender, about 2 minutes. Using tongs, transfer the shrimp to a plate and set aside. Add the onion, bell pepper, celery, and a pinch each of salt and black pepper to the pan and sauté until soft, 7 to 10 minutes. Add tomato paste and garlic and cook, stirring continuously, for 2 minutes. Add the sherry, scraping up any tomato paste stuck to the bottom of the pan, and let the sherry reduce for about 30 seconds.

3 Add the stock, bay leaf, Worcestershire, 1 tea-spoon salt, the sugar, and the Tabasco. Simmer over medium-low heat for 15 to 20 minutes, until the sauce reduces and thickens slightly. Taste and add a few more dashes of Tabasco and a pinch of salt if needed. Return the shrimp to the pan, stir to coat with the sauce, and cook for 2 to 3 minutes. Remove the bay leaf. Serve over warm rice, topped with the parsley.

BUTTER-BASTED FILLET OF FISH

with Salsa Verde

Don't let cooking fish intimidate you. This butter-basted fish is so easy, you don't even have to worry about that nerve-racking flip that might leave your fish in pieces. The butter does the work to cook and flavor your fish and make it extra juicy. Change this dish up by using Chilean sea bass.

SERVES 2

Salsa Verde

1 cup loosely packed fresh flat-leaf parsley leaves

¼ cup loosely packed fresh oregano leaves

½ cup loosely packed fresh mint leaves

1 tablespoon capers

1 tablespoon finely chopped shallot

2 tablespoons white balsamic vinegar

½ teaspoon kosher salt

¼ teaspoon freshly ground black pepper

5 tablespoons olive oil

Fish

2 (7- to 8-ounce) skinless black cod fillets, 1 to 2 inches thick

½ teaspoon kosher salt

¼ teaspoon freshly ground black pepper

2 tablespoons olive oil

4 tablespoons (½ stick) butter, cubed

2 garlic cloves, smashed and peeled

2 sprigs oregano

1 **MAKE THE SALSA VERDE:** In a mini food processor, combine the parsley, oregano, mint, capers, shallot, vinegar, salt, and pepper. Pulse 2 or 3 times to chop the herbs. Add the olive oil and pulse 3 or 4 times to combine. The oil should turn to a cloudy lime-green color. Transfer to a serving bowl and set aside.

2 **MAKE THE FISH:** Take the fish out of the fridge 15 minutes prior to cooking to come to room temperature. This will make it cook more evenly. Season the fillets on both sides with the salt and pepper.

3 In a medium nonstick pan, heat the olive oil over medium-high heat until shimmering, about 2 minutes. Add the fish to the pan and sear on the skinned side for 1 minute. Add the butter and allow it to melt for 30 seconds, then add the garlic and oregano to the pan. The herbs will pop and sizzle at first as the moisture cooks out of them. Tilt the pan slightly away from you so the butter can collect at the far end of the pan. Then, using a big metal tablespoon, like a serving spoon, scoop up some butter, level the pan, and baste the fish with the butter. Continue basting the fish continuously for 4 to 5 minutes. The butter should be hot and bubbling while you're basting, and the fish will slowly become whiter and opaque in color as it cooks.

4 Reduce the heat to very low and cover. Braise until the fish is cooked through, 5 to 8 minutes, depending on the thickness of your fillets. The fish is done when it easily flakes from the corner with a fork. The edges should be the tiniest bit browned and buttery and the fish should be soft and flaky when you cut into it.

5 Using a spatula, gently lift the fillets from the pan onto individual serving plates and drizzle each with some salsa verde.

 Trisha's Tip

Salsa verde is an Italian-style fresh herb green sauce that adds a bright fresh pop to your fish and is also great on roasted vegetables, spread on a sandwich, or even on a steak!

BETH'S SHRIMP & GRITS

Every self-respecting Southerner has some kind of shrimp-and-grits recipe in their arsenal. I think it's a law! And everybody thinks theirs is the best, but Beth's shrimp and grits are the best, really! This creamy, cheesy shrimp-and-andouille-sausage combo brings together everything I love about Southern fare. The addition of tomatoes takes this Southern coastal classic up a notch.

SERVES 4

2¼ cups chicken stock

Kosher salt

1 cup yellow corn grits

Freshly ground black pepper

¼ teaspoon cayenne pepper

¼ cup whole milk

½ cup heavy cream

½ cup grated Monterey Jack cheese

½ cup grated mild cheddar cheese

¼ cup grated Parmesan cheese

3 tablespoons butter

1 pound medium shrimp (about 40), peeled and deveined

2 teaspoons Cajun seasoning (with salt in the blend)

½ pound andouille sausage, thinly sliced

5 green onions (white and green parts separated), sliced

½ shallot, minced

1 cup grape tomatoes, halved

2 tablespoons dry sherry or white wine

2 tablespoons all-purpose flour

1 lemon, quartered

Tabasco sauce

1 In a medium saucepan, combine 1½ cups of the stock, 1 cup water, and a large pinch of salt. Bring to a boil, then whisk in the grits, ¼ teaspoon black pepper, and the cayenne. Reduce the heat to low and cook, stirring regularly, until the grits are cooked, about 10 minutes. Stir in the milk, heavy cream, cheeses, and 2 tablespoons of the butter. Remove from the heat and cover to keep warm.

2 Season the shrimp with the Cajun seasoning and a pinch of pepper and set aside on a plate while you cook the sausage.

3 In a large skillet, sear the sausage on both sides over medium-high heat, 5 to 6 minutes, then set aside on a plate.

4 Add the remaining 1 tablespoon butter to the pan, reduce the heat to medium, and add the whites of the green onions and the shallot. Cook until fragrant and softened, about 2 minutes, then add the tomatoes and cook for another minute or two, until they begin to soften.

5 Add the shrimp and sear on both sides, about 4 minutes total. Transfer the shrimp-and-tomato mixture to the plate with sausage. Pour the sherry into the pan and cook, scraping up any brown bits on the bottom of the pan, until mostly reduced, about 1 minute.

6 In a small bowl, stir together the flour and 2 tablespoons of the stock, then stir in the remaining stock (should be ¾ cup in total).

7 Pour the stock mixture into the skillet and simmer for another minute, until it starts to thicken. Stir in the sausage, shrimp, and tomatoes. Season with a sprinkle of salt.

8 Serve warm bowls of grits topped with the shrimp and sausage mix. Top each serving with a squeeze of lemon and the greens of the green onions, and serve with hot sauce on the side.

CORNFLAKE-FRIED CATFISH

I grew up on a farm with a small pond that was home to lots of catfish. Mama would always fry up whatever we caught, and make homemade hush puppies and fries to go alongside. It's such a good memory of great food and wonderful family time. Sometimes she would crush up corn flakes as an alternative to cornmeal to give a little sweet crunch to the fish. These flavorful, crunchy catfish strips are a nod to her. If you like, serve with tartar sauce instead of my spicy remoulade. We love you and we miss you, Mama!

SERVES 4

Spicy Remoulade

1 cup mayonnaise

2 tablespoons hot vinegar peppers, drained and finely chopped, plus 2 tablespoons pepper juice from the jar

2 teaspoons sweet paprika

1 teaspoon sugar

1 tablespoon finely chopped fresh parsley leaves

½ teaspoon kosher salt

Catfish

Vegetable oil, for frying

3 (5- to 6-ounce) catfish fillets

Kosher salt

10 cups cornflakes (one 12-ounce box)

1 cup all-purpose flour

½ teaspoon freshly ground black pepper

1 teaspoon smoked paprika

1 teaspoon onion powder

1 teaspoon garlic powder

¼ teaspoon cayenne pepper

2 large eggs

⅓ cup buttermilk

1 tablespoon yellow mustard

Hot sauce (I like Tabasco), for serving

1 **MAKE THE REMOULADE:** In a small bowl, mix together the mayonnaise, peppers and their juice, paprika, sugar, parsley, and salt and set aside.

2 **MAKE THE CATFISH:** Fill a Dutch oven with 3 inches of oil. Clip a deep-fry thermometer to its side and heat the oil over high heat to 360°F. Fit a rimmed baking sheet with a wire rack and set it nearby.

3 Meanwhile, cutting against the grain, slice the catfish fillets into 5- to 6-inch strips, 1 to 1½ inches wide, then season lightly with salt on both sides.

4 Put the cornflakes in a resealable plastic bag, then use a rolling pin to crush them into smaller flakes.

5 Set up a dredging station with three shallow bowls. In one bowl, whisk together the flour, 1 teaspoon salt, the pepper, paprika, onion powder, garlic powder, and cayenne. In the second bowl, whisk together the eggs, buttermilk, and mustard. Put the crushed cornflakes in the third bowl.

6 Dip each catfish strip in the flour mixture with one dry hand and shake it off. Then, with your other hand, dip the strip in the egg mixture, shaking off any excess, and add it to the cornflakes. With your dry hand, press the cornflakes into the fish and then set the cornflake-crusted fish on a plate while you dredge the rest.

7 Working in batches of 4 or 5 strips at a time, fry the fish in the hot oil for 3 to 4 minutes, until the catfish feels rigid and is dark golden brown and cooked through. Place on the rack and sprinkle with a little salt. Repeat to fry the remaining fish.

8 Serve with the remoulade sauce and a dash of your favorite hot sauce.

TRISHA'S TIP

Pie plates are great to use for dredging fried foods. Designating one of your hands as the dry hand and one as the wet helps get the dredging job done easier!

Veggie Night

Garth and I created veggie night years ago, when
our daughters, Taylor, August, and Allie, were younger. Our goal
was to get more vegetables into their lives, which we did, but
we came up with so many tasty recipes, we had the girls actually
asking for veggie night! That's a win in my book. Everything
in this chapter is vegetarian, but you don't have to be vegetarian
to enjoy hearty dishes like mushroom tacos and homemade
gnocchi. You'll find yourself making these recipes just
because your family loves them!

GRILLED YELLOW GAZPACHO

I have to admit I was late to the party on gazpacho, which by definition is just a cold soup made of raw blended vegetables. I grew up in a house where soup was always served hot, so I was a little wary of this Spanish concoction. When my niece Ashley bought her first home, I made her a special meal to celebrate. She wanted gazpacho. All I can say is, wow! The yellow tomatoes make this soup beautiful, and it's just packed with flavor. This gazpacho has now become one of my favorite soups of all time, especially in the summer. Here's to trying something new! Thanks, Ashley!

SERVES 4 TO 6

2¼ pounds ripe yellow tomatoes

1 large yellow pepper, halved

1 small garlic clove, peeled

1 small shallot, halved

1 tablespoon white wine vinegar

Kosher salt and freshly ground black pepper

1 English cucumber, peeled and halved

¼ cup olive oil, plus more for drizzling

½ cup torn fresh basil leaves

1   Heat a grill to medium-high or heat a grill pan over medium-high heat. Grill the tomatoes and half the bell pepper, turning occasionally, until lightly charred on all sides, about 5 minutes.

2   Transfer to a blender and add the garlic, shallot, vinegar, salt, black pepper, and half the cucumber. Puree until very smooth. With the motor running, slowly add the olive oil and blend until combined. Strain through a medium-mesh sieve into a bowl. Cover and chill for at least 4 hours or up to overnight. Finely chop the remaining bell pepper and cucumber and keep refrigerated.

3   Before serving, season the gazpacho with salt and black pepper to taste. Ladle into bowls and top with the diced pepper and cucumber, then drizzle with olive oil and sprinkle with the basil.

If you have a high-powered blender like a Vitamix that will power-blend your soup, you can skip the straining part.

English cucumbers are long and slender. Their skins are thinner than those of regular cucumbers, so there's no need to peel. They're usually advertised as seedless, though they do have undeveloped seeds, which makes them great for salads and garnishing gazpacho.

SUNRISE CITRUS BEET SALAD

I've lived in Nashville now off and on for over thirty years. I came here to try to make my music dreams come true. I am so grateful, and I know how lucky I am to be able to make music for a living! I may have come to this city because of my love for music, but I fell in love with Nashville for its sense of community. This really is a town that comes together when the going gets tough, and I'm proud to be a part of it. One noteworthy organization that I support is the Nashville Food Project, led by my friend Tallu Schuyler Quinn. Their mission is to bring people together to grow, cook, and share nourishing food, with the goals of cultivating community and alleviating hunger in our city. Beth and I made a version of this beautiful and tasty salad for one of the project's causes: a community center in town that helps those who need it. The food was wonderful, but being a part of the community in a way that gives back feeds the soul. I encourage you to find a group like this that you can be a part of in your own community! Check out TheNashvilleFoodProject.org for information on this wonderful organization.

SERVES 4

1 pound golden beets, leaves removed

1 pound red beets, leaves removed

½ cup olive oil

Kosher salt and freshly cracked black pepper

1 large navel orange

1 pink grapefruit

¼ cup champagne vinegar

2 tablespoons honey

¼ cup fresh mint leaves, torn

¼ cup hazelnuts, toasted and roughly chopped

4 ounces feta cheese, crumbled

1 Preheat the oven to 400°F.

2 Place the beets on a large piece of aluminum foil. Drizzle with 2 tablespoons of the olive oil and sprinkle generously with salt and pepper. Peel the orange all the way down to the flesh and tuck the peels among the beets; set the peeled orange aside. Fold the foil up and around the beets to create a closed packet. Place the packet on a baking sheet and roast until the beets are tender when pierced with a paring knife and the edges of the orange peels have begun to caramelize, 45 to 50 minutes. Open the packet carefully and discard the orange peels. Let the beets cool slightly, about 10 minutes.

3 Meanwhile, peel the grapefruit down to the flesh and slice into ¼-inch-thick rounds, then cut them into bite-size segments. Repeat with the peeled orange.

4 In a small bowl, whisk together the vinegar, remaining 6 tablespoons olive oil, the honey, and a pinch each of salt and pepper. Set aside.

5 Once the beets have cooled slightly, hold them in a paper towel and use the edge of a paring knife to peel off the skins. Slice the beets into bite-size pieces, place the two colors in separate medium bowls so they don't bleed into each other. Add half the vinaigrette to each bowl of beets and toss to coat, then arrange them on a platter, alternating with the cut citrus, and top with the mint leaves, hazelnuts, and feta.

Trisha's Tip

If you are going to get this salad ready now but plan to serve it later, keep your beets marinating separately in the vinaigrette, and when you're ready to serve, combine everything. The beets can marinate covered in the refrigerator for up to 2 days before serving.

GRILLED ROMAINE

with Creamy Parmesan Ranch

This gorgeous grilled hearts-of-romaine salad combines the flavors of a Caesar salad with the crunch of a big wedge. If the thought of little furry anchovies freaks you out, just remember that you're pulverizing the dressing in a blender, so don't panic! And have you ever heard of umami? Umami is an almost indescribable fifth taste. Yep. There's salty, sweet, sour, bitter, and umami, which is such a satisfying savory taste that you'll find yourself wanting to eat it over and over (like a bag of potato chips!). And—you guessed it—anchovies are an umami food. What you'll taste in the bold Parmesan ranch dressing is salty and savory, but the magic of umami will have you feeling all food-happy. Trust me on this one! And if you are vegetarian, just leave out the anchovies; the Parmesan will still make it taste great!

SERVES 4

Dressing

½ cup plain low-fat Greek yogurt

3 tablespoons olive oil

2 tablespoons fresh lemon juice

2 teaspoons Dijon mustard

2 anchovy fillets (see Note)

1 garlic clove, chopped

½ cup grated Parmesan cheese

Kosher salt and freshly ground black pepper

Salad

3 tablespoons olive oil

2 garlic cloves, smashed and peeled

2 romaine lettuce hearts, halved lengthwise

1½ cups cubed stale crusty bread, such as a baguette (about 4 inches of baguette)

Kosher salt and freshly ground black pepper

Grated Parmesan cheese, for topping

1 **MAKE THE DRESSING:** In a blender, combine the yogurt, oil, lemon juice, mustard, anchovies, garlic, and 3 tablespoons water and blend until smooth. Add the Parmesan and pulse to combine, then season with salt and pepper to taste.

2 **MAKE THE SALAD:** In a large skillet, heat the olive oil over medium heat. Add the garlic and cook, stirring, until aromatic and golden, about 3 minutes. Remove the garlic. Brush the cut sides of the lettuce halves with some of the garlicky oil.

3 Add the bread cubes to the skillet with the remaining oil and cook, stirring often, until golden brown on all sides, about 5 minutes. Transfer to a bowl and season lightly with salt and pepper.

4 Heat a large double-burner grill pan over medium-high heat. Season the lettuce with salt and pepper. Grill the cut side of the lettuce until marked and just starting to wilt, about 3 minutes.

5 Serve the lettuce and croutons drizzled with the dressing and topped with Parmesan. Unused dressing will keep in an airtight container in the refrigerator for up to 1 week.

BUTTERNUT SQUASH & HOMINY SUCCOTASH

Hominy is corn that's been soaked in an alkali solution to loosen the hull. It's a little chewy and has a very earthy flavor. It's sometimes used to make tortillas and tamales, which is why, to me, it tastes a lot like a corn tortilla! Cooked together with Brussels sprouts and butternut squash, hominy makes this savory succotash the ultimate veggie dish that can be served as a side or a meal on its own.

Try substituting sweet Peppadew peppers for the roasted red peppers. You can find them canned, or fresh if your grocery store has a good olive bar. Roughly chop them and add 2 tablespoons of the pickling juice in place of the apple cider vinegar for variety.

SERVES 4 TO 6

4 tablespoons (½ stick) butter

3 cups diced (½-inch pieces) butternut squash

6 ounces small Brussels sprouts, trimmed and quartered (about 2 cups)

1 cup frozen baby lima beans, thawed

Kosher salt and freshly ground black pepper

1 (15.5-ounce) can yellow or white hominy, drained and rinsed

¼ cup roasted red peppers, diced

2 tablespoons apple cider vinegar

This succotash is great the next day, warmed up with a fried egg on top and some hot sauce drizzled over it.

1   Warm a large high-sided saucepan over medium heat, then add 3 tablespoons of the butter and warm until the butter begins to foam and just brown, about 2 minutes. Toss in the squash, Brussels sprouts, and lima beans and sauté on all sides, stirring occasionally and taking care to give the vegetables time to brighten a little in color, for 15 minutes.

2   Sprinkle in ½ teaspoon salt and a big pinch of black pepper and stir. Add the remaining 1 tablespoon butter and the hominy and cook until the squash and Brussels sprouts are fork-tender, about 5 minutes more.

3   Stir in the roasted red peppers and vinegar, then taste and add more salt and black pepper if needed. Serve warm.

HARD CIDER CHEESE SOUP

with Sautéed Apples & Pretzel Croutons

At the first signs of fall in Tennessee—a cool breeze, the start of leaves changing color, the first outdoor bonfire—I crave soup. This cheesy cider soup ticks all the boxes. With three kinds of cheeses, caramelized apples, and crunchy pretzel bites, there's so much to love about this hearty soup. You'll be ready for sweater weather!

SERVES 4 TO 6

Garnish

4 tablespoons (½ stick) butter, at room temperature

2 Gala or Honeycrisp apples, peeled, cored, and diced into ½-inch pieces

2 soft pretzel rolls, sliced ¼ inch thick

Soup

4 tablespoons (½ stick) butter

1 medium sweet onion (I like Vidalia), grated

3 medium carrots (about 6 ounces), grated

Kosher salt and freshly ground black pepper

2 garlic cloves, minced

1 (12-ounce) bottle dry hard cider

2½ cups vegetable stock

2 tablespoons all-purpose flour

Pinch of ground cloves

1 cup heavy cream

1 (8-ounce) package cream cheese, cut into small chunks

8 ounces mild cheddar cheese, grated

8 ounces Colby Jack cheese, grated

1 **MAKE THE GARNISH:** Preheat the oven to 400°F. Place a cold baking sheet on the middle rack to preheat.

2 In a medium skillet, melt 2 tablespoons of the butter over medium heat. Add the apples. Spread the apples out in an even layer and let them caramelize on all sides, about 8 minutes. Set aside.

3 Spread the remaining 2 tablespoons butter on the pretzel roll slices. Remove the preheated pan from the oven. Carefully add the pretzel slices to the pan and toast in the oven for 3 minutes, then flip and toast until lightly golden brown, 3 minutes more. Set aside to cool.

4 **MAKE THE SOUP:** In a large soup pot, melt 2 tablespoons of the butter over medium-high heat. Add the onions, carrots, ½ teaspoon salt, and a pinch of pepper and sauté until tender, about 5 minutes. Add the garlic and cook for another minute, until fragrant. Stir in the cider and stock and bring to a boil, then reduce the heat to maintain a steady simmer and cook for 10 minutes.

5 While the soup is simmering, in a medium saucepan, melt the remaining 2 tablespoons butter over medium heat. Stir in the flour and cook until there's a light toasted fragrance, about 2 minutes, to make a light roux. Add the cloves and slowly whisk in the cream, making sure to break up any lumps. Keep stirring, making sure to not scorch the pan, until the cream thickens, about 3 minutes. Turn off the heat and slowly whisk ½ cup of the soup into the thickened cream. (This will smooth the cream so it doesn't get lumpy when you add it to the soup.)

6 Reduce the heat under the soup to low and whisk in the thinned cream mixture. Add the cream cheese, cheddar, and Colby Jack and stir until well blended. Using an immersion blender, carefully blend the soup directly in the pot for 2 to 3 minutes, until smooth (or carefully transfer the soup to a stand blender and blend until smooth).

7 Serve the soup with a spoonful of apple on top and some pretzel toasts on the side.

TRISHA's TIP

I like using a high-powered blender like a Vitamix to completely blend this soup into cheesy, creamy magic. Remember to slowly and carefully pour hot soup into a blender, vent the lid slightly, and cover the lid with a dish towel to prevent splashing.

GRILLED TOMATO & ZUCCHINI SALAD

with Goat Cheese Croutons

I know I'm lucky to have grown up on a farm, and one of things I'm most grateful for is the wonderful garden we grew every year. If you've ever grown a garden, you know that there's a period of time in midsummer when tomato season overlaps zucchini season! If you're very lucky, your garden will yield a lot of each vegetable. I love this easy grilled salad that uses my garden bounty. The goat cheese croutons are a nice touch, and since they're baked in a packet on your grill, you get all the flavor without having to fry anything up.

SERVES 4

1 egg

1 cup panko bread crumbs

1 teaspoon dry ranch dressing mix

6 tablespoons extra-virgin olive oil

6 ounces goat cheese, cold from the fridge

3 beefsteak tomatoes, cut into ½-inch-thick slices

3 small to medium green and yellow zucchini, cut at an angle into ¼-inch-thick slices

1 tablespoon fresh thyme leaves

2 teaspoons kosher salt

1 teaspoon freshly cracked black pepper

1 bunch green onions, trimmed

1 lemon, halved

1 cup store-bought candied pecans

1   Preheat a grill to 400°F.

2   Beat the egg in a small bowl. In a second bowl, toss the panko, ranch mix, and 1 teaspoon of the olive oil. Cut the goat cheese into 10 pieces and roll each into a ball. Dip the goat cheese in the egg, letting any excess drip off, and then in the panko mix, pressing it into the cheese to adhere and reshaping them into discs.

3   Pull a 24-inch-long sheet of heavy-duty aluminum foil and then fold it in half lengthwise. Open it up, brush the foil with a little olive oil, and line up the breaded goat cheese discs on one side, then pinch the edges of the foil closed and

cut a small slit on the side to vent steam. Slide the packet onto a corner of the grill and cook with the lid of the grill open for 15 to 17 minutes, flipping the foil pack gently halfway through.

4   Meanwhile, put the tomatoes and zucchini in a large bowl and toss with 2 tablespoons of the olive oil, the thyme, salt, and pepper. Place on the grill alongside the foil packet and grill until all the vegetables have grill marks and are a bit charred, 2 to 3 minutes per side.

5   After you get the tomatoes and zucchini on the grill, immediately add the green onions to the bowl, coating them in the remaining oil and seasoning, then get them on the grill alongside the other veggies and grill for 4 to 5 minutes.

6   Transfer the grilled tomatoes and zucchini to a serving platter and add a generous squeeze of lemon juice and a drizzle of olive oil.

7   Transfer the green onions to a cutting board and chop into 1-inch-long sticks, both greens and whites, and sprinkle them onto the salad.

8   Once the goat cheese is baked, slide the packet onto a cutting board and carefully tear open the top. Garnish the salad with the goat cheese croutons, top with the candied pecans, and serve.

MUSHROOM POBLANO TACOS

Poblanos are mild chile peppers used most often in Mexican and Tex-Mex cooking. They're not super spicy, but they have a really great flavor, especially when charred for these tacos. My friends and fellow musicians Amanda Shires and Jason Isbell came over for lunch one day, and I wanted to make something special for them. Knowing they love Tex-Mex food, I settled on charring the poblanos and pairing them with sautéed mushrooms, all in warm corn tortillas. Amanda and Jason loved them, and we had no leftovers! I suggest putting out the toppings in separate little bowls so your guests can top their tacos however they choose.

SERVES 4

2 medium poblano peppers

2 tablespoons olive oil

1½ pounds mixed mushrooms (such as cremini, shiitake, and oyster), sliced

Kosher salt and freshly ground black pepper

½ teaspoon ground coriander

2 garlic cloves, minced

¼ cup chopped fresh cilantro, plus more for serving

1 tablespoon fresh lime juice, plus lime wedges for serving

12 corn tortillas, warmed

Thinly sliced radishes, for serving

Diced avocado, for serving

Crumbled queso fresco, for serving

Mexican crema or sour cream, for serving

1 Use tongs to roast the poblanos over the open flame of a gas stovetop burner, turning them occasionally, until well charred on all sides, about 4 minutes. Put in a bowl, cover with a clean dish towel or plastic wrap, and let stand for 5 minutes. Peel the poblanos with a knife, scraping off the skin, then remove the stem and seeds. Cut the flesh crosswise into thin strips and set aside.

2 In a large skillet, heat the olive oil over medium-high heat. Add the mushrooms, sprinkle with salt and black pepper, and cook, stirring occasionally, until they have released some of their liquid and are golden brown, about 10 minutes.

3 Add the poblano strips, coriander, and garlic and cook, stirring, until the garlic is fragrant, about 1 minute. Add the cilantro and lime juice and season with salt to taste.

4 Serve the mushroom poblano filling in warm tortillas, topped with radishes, avocado, queso fresco, crema, and more cilantro, with lime wedges alongside.

TRISHA'S TIP

If you don't have a gas cooktop, place the peppers on a baking sheet and broil them, turning every few minutes, until completely blackened on all sides. You can also char them on an outdoor grill.

HOMEMADE GNOCCHI

with Two Sauces

Garth and I end up in Los Angeles a good bit for TV shows and live performances. If we have an evening off, we like to take advantage of one of the many amazing restaurants LA has to offer. We used to frequent an Italian restaurant on Pico Boulevard called Anna's. The staff there was so friendly, the atmosphere was perfection, and the food was incredible. Garth especially loved their gnocchi, which they served with two sauces, one red and one white. Anna's is gone now, closed in 2010, but I'll always remember them for their kindness and great Italian fare. My tomato and creamy mushroom sauces are my homage to this classic Italian restaurant.

SERVES 4 TO 6

3 medium russet potatoes (about 1½ pounds total)

Kosher salt

1 large egg, beaten

1¼ to 1½ cups all-purpose flour, plus more for dusting

Creamy Porcini Mushroom Sauce and/or Cherry Tomato Red Sauce (page 177), for serving

Grated Parmesan cheese, for serving

Fresh basil, for garnish

1 Place the potatoes in a large saucepan with enough water to cover by an inch. Bring to a simmer over medium heat and cook until tender all the way through when pierced with a knife, about 20 minutes. Drain and let cool slightly.

2 When the potatoes are still hot but you are able to handle them, peel off the skins with a paring knife and press the warm potatoes through a ricer onto a working surface. Spread them into an even layer and let cool completely.

3 Sprinkle the cooled potatoes with 1 teaspoon salt and drizzle with the beaten egg. Sprinkle with 1 cup of the flour and use your hands (or preferably a bench scraper, if you have one) to mix and knead the dough together. Add ¼ to ½ cup more flour as needed until the dough holds together and is only slightly sticky. (A good way to tell if the dough is the right texture is to cut the dough ball in half. The interior should look like cookie dough peppered with small holes throughout.)

4 Bring a pot of water to a boil and salt it generously. Dust a rimmed baking sheet with flour. To form the gnocchi, break off a piece of dough and roll it into a log about ¾ inch thick, keeping your hands and counter well floured as you work. Cut the log crosswise into ¾-inch segments. Give each piece a quick single roll between your palms to round them slightly. Roll each piece off the back of the floured tines of a fork, pressing with your thumb as you roll down to make a small indentation on one side and ridges from the fork on the other side. Place on the prepared baking sheet.

5 In two batches, add the gnocchi to the boiling water and cook for 2 to 4 minutes, until cooked through. Drain.

6 Serve tossed in the sauce of your choosing, garnished with Parmesan and basil.

TRISHA'S TIPS

To cook potatoes in a pressure cooker, sprinkle salt over the potatoes and follow the manufacturer's instructions to cook for 5 minutes. Release the pressure immediately, then drain the potatoes and let cool.

Cold potatoes are almost impossible to push through a ricer. Make sure you handle them as hot as your hands can stand!

Recipe Continues

TRISHA'S TIP

Extra uncooked gnocchi can be frozen. Freeze them on the floured baking sheet until solid, then pack them into plastic resealable bags and freeze for up to 2 months. When ready to use, cook using the same method for fresh. Don't allow them to thaw out before cooking, or they could fall apart.

Creamy Porcini Mushroom Sauce

½ ounce dried porcini mushrooms

Kosher salt

1 pound uncooked gnocchi (see page 173; ½ recipe)

2 tablespoons butter

2 tablespoons fresh oregano leaves

½ cup heavy cream

½ teaspoon freshly ground black pepper

¼ cup grated Pecorino Romano cheese

2 tablespoons chopped fresh flat-leaf parsley, for garnish

Place the mushrooms in a heatproof bowl and pour in enough boiling water to cover them. Let them hydrate for 5 minutes.

Bring a medium saucepan of water to a boil and salt it generously. Cook the gnocchi as directed on page 173, the drain and set aside.

Drain the porcinis, saving ¼ cup of the soaking liquid, and roughly chop the mushrooms.

In a medium sauté pan, melt the butter over medium-low heat, then add the chopped mushrooms and oregano and sauté for 3 to 4 minutes.

In a high-sided skillet, combine the reserved porcini water, the cream, pepper, and ¼ teaspoon salt. Bring the mixture to a simmer, being careful not to let it boil, and cook for 4 minutes, or until slightly thickened. Stir in the mushrooms and reduce the heat to low. Add the gnocchi to the pan and coat with the sauce, then serve, topped with the Romano cheese and garnished with the parsley.

Serves 4

Pecorino Romano cheese is a little tangier than Parmesan, but substituting Parmesan is fine!

Cherry Tomato Red Sauce

Kosher salt

12 ounces cherry tomatoes

3 sprigs thyme

¼ cup olive oil

Freshly ground black pepper

1 pound uncooked gnocchi (see page page 173; ½ recipe)

1 tablespoon tomato paste

2 garlic cloves, finely grated

2 tablespoons butter

Small block of Parmesan cheese, to shave over the gnocchi

Bring a medium pot of water to a boil and salt it generously.

In a medium skillet, combine the cherry tomatoes, thyme, and olive oil. Shake the pan to coat the tomatoes. Cook over medium-high heat; as the olive oil heats up, the tomatoes and thyme will start to sizzle and the tomatoes will burst. Sprinkle with ¾ teaspoon salt and a pinch of pepper and cook, gently stirring occasionally, until most of the tomatoes have blistered and burst, about 5 minutes.

Add the gnocchi to the pot of boiling water and cook for 3 to 4 minutes. Reserve ¼ cup of the cooking water, then drain.

Give the tomatoes a little press with the back of a spoon and add the tomato paste and garlic. Cook, stirring, for 1 minute, or until the garlic is fragrant. Add the reserved gnocchi cooking water and stir. Cook at a low simmer for 3 to 4 minutes, until the water reduces by about half.

Discard the thyme stems and taste the sauce to see if it needs a little more salt and pepper; adjust if needed. Add the butter, stirring it quickly to melt and blend into the sauce.

Add the cooked gnocchi to the pan and coat in the warm sauce. Serve with plenty of freshly shaved Parmesan.

Serves 4

The starchy gnocchi cooking water is what really brings this sauce together.

MAGIC BROTH VEGETABLE SOUP

Warm vegetable soup truly soothes the soul! But if I'm honest, for me, it's all about the homemade broth. I give you permission to use store-bought in this recipe, but I really encourage you to spend an afternoon making a batch of this antioxidant-rich broth to freeze and use any time you need a pick-me-up in your soups and stews. From the onions and radishes to the ginger and mushrooms, there are so many immunity-boosting foods in the broth to cheer up your body and soul.

SERVES 6

---

4 cups vegetable stock, store-bought or homemade (recipe follows)

2 (14-ounce) cans fire-roasted diced tomatoes with their juices

4 Yukon gold potatoes, diced

1 (11-ounce) can extra-sweet canned corn kernels, drained

1 (10-ounce) bag frozen green peas

Kosher salt and freshly ground black pepper

In a medium saucepan, combine the stock, tomatoes, potatoes, corn, and peas. Bring to a boil, then reduce the heat to medium and simmer for 20 minutes, or until the potatoes are cooked through and tender. Season with salt and pepper to taste and serve.

Trisha's Tips

Leaving the vegetables for the broth unpeeled while they cook releases the most nutrients into the broth; just make sure they are cleaned well before adding them to the pot.

I add vegetable bouillon for more flavor. You can leave it out; just make sure to check the seasoning as the broth cooks and season with salt and pepper to taste as you go.

When making the broth, if the liquid starts to reduce too much, add more water.

Homemade Vegetable Broth

1 large sweet onion (I like Vidalia), unpeeled, quartered

1 large carrot, unpeeled, cut into thirds

1 leek, white and green parts, halved

1 celery stalk, roughly chopped

1 sweet potato, unpeeled, chopped into chunks

1 turnip and its greens, chopped

½ cup radishes, chopped

1 small bunch parsley, torn

2 sprigs thyme

4 large garlic cloves, smashed but not peeled

7 whole black peppercorns

1 bay leaf

1 (1-inch) piece fresh ginger, unpeeled, cut in half

4 ounces shiitake mushrooms

1½ teaspoons kosher salt, plus more as needed

2 vegetable bouillon cubes

Freshly ground black pepper

In a large stockpot, combine the onion, carrot, leek, celery, sweet potato, turnip and turnip greens, radishes, parsley, thyme, garlic, peppercorns, bay leaf, ginger, and mushrooms. Add the salt, bouillon cubes, and 4 quarts water. Cover and bring to a boil. Remove the lid, reduce the heat to low, and simmer for 3 to 4 hours.

Strain the broth through a large strainer into a clean large pot. Season with salt and pepper to taste. Allow to cool completely and store in airtight containers in the refrigerator for up to 1 week or freeze for up to 4 months.

Makes 12 cups

SAVORY POTATO FETA GALETTE

A *galette* is a French term for, basically, a flat pie. It can be filled with a sweet or savory filling, so it's super versatile. My favorite thing about a galette is that when you roll out the dough, it doesn't have to be perfect. No fancy shape or masterful crimping of the crust required. Just top the dough and fold the edges over. It's rustic-looking, but beautiful! One of my favorite fillings for a galette is this savory potato-and-feta mixture, drizzled with yummy balsamic glaze!

SERVES 4 TO 6

Crust

2½ cups sifted all-purpose flour, plus more for dusting

1 teaspoon sugar

½ teaspoon kosher salt

1 cup plus 2 tablespoons (2¼ sticks) unsalted butter, cubed and chilled

½ cup ice water

Filling

3 medium Yukon gold potatoes (about ¾ pound total)

1 teaspoon fresh thyme leaves

2 tablespoons butter, melted

Kosher salt and freshly ground black pepper

2 tablespoons Kalamata olives, pitted and split

2 ounces feta cheese, crumbled (¼ cup)

2 tablespoons extra-virgin olive oil

1 egg, beaten

Store-bought balsamic glaze, for drizzling

1 **MAKE THE CRUST:** In a large bowl, whisk together the flour, sugar, and salt to combine. Add the butter to the bowl and use a pastry cutter or two knives to cut the butter into the flour mixture until pea-size lumps form.

2 Sprinkle in the ice water 1 tablespoon at a time, using a fork or your hands to bring the dough together, until it becomes just sticky enough to form into a ball. You may not need to use all the ice water—use just enough to make the dough stick together.

3 Transfer the dough to a clean work surface dusted with flour. Press all the moistened portions together gently and quickly with your fingers. Do not knead. The less the dough is handled, the more tender and flakier the pastry will be. Form the dough into a disc and wrap with plastic wrap. Refrigerate for at least 1 hour. (This step can be done several days in advance.)

4 Preheat the oven to 400°F. Line a rimmed baking sheet with parchment paper.

5 **MAKE THE FILLING:** Slice the potatoes into ⅛-inch-thick rounds, put them in a large bowl, and toss with the thyme, melted butter, and a pinch each of salt and pepper.

6 Spread in one layer on the prepared baking sheet and roast for 10 minutes. The potatoes will be golden in color and curled on the edges when done. Remove the potatoes from the oven and let cool while you roll out the dough. Reduce the oven temperature to 375°F. Line a rimmed baking sheet with parchment paper (or use the baking sheet you cooked your potatoes on—just make sure it has cooled down completely).

7 Roll out the dough to just shy of ¼ inch thick and trim the edges to make a 14-inch round, then place on the parchment-lined baking sheet. Using a fork, add a few holes throughout the dough so it won't puff up in the middle as it bakes.

8 Leave a 2-inch border around the perimeter of
the dough and begin to fill the center. Start by
overlapping the potatoes in concentric circles
from the center out. Then sprinkle the olives and
feta over the top. Drizzle the olive oil over the
filling, then fold the edges of the dough over onto
the filling, allowing the folds to overlap each
other. Brush the dough with the egg, getting it
in between the overlapping folds to help lock it
together.

9 Sprinkle the egg-washed dough with a little salt
and pepper and bake for 35 to 40 minutes, until
the dough has turned golden brown, rotating
halfway through baking.

10 Let cool for 10 minutes, then drizzle with
balsamic glaze and serve.

CREAMY SWEET CORN SPINACH ENCHILADAS

My chef friend Michelle shared this incredible vegetarian enchilada casserole with me and I couldn't be happier! This style of creamy enchiladas is called *enchiladas suizas,* which literally means "Swiss enchiladas." Some attribute the name to the large amount of cheese and cream in this dish resembling the Swiss Alps. Michelle took a trip to Switzerland last year and after eating so much melted cheese there, she understood how the name came about! I love it when cultures exchange food traditions. Swiss immigrants in Mexico mingled their culinary traditions with those of their new country, and we are the lucky recipients of those integrated food cultures!

SERVES 4 TO 6

1½ cups green salsa

¾ cup Mexican crema or sour cream

2 tablespoons vegetable oil

1 small onion, diced small

1 garlic clove, thinly sliced

¾ cup fresh or frozen sweet corn kernels, thawed if frozen

½ (8-ounce) package cream cheese, at room temperature

½ teaspoon ground cumin

¼ teaspoon freshly ground black pepper

10 ounces baby spinach

12 ounces Mexican-style shredded cheese blend

15 soft corn tortillas

Leaves from 1 bunch cilantro, chopped

Hot sauce, for serving

1 In a medium bowl, whisk together the salsa and crema and set aside for the flavors to meld while you make the filling.

2 Warm a large skillet over medium-high heat and add the oil. Swirl the oil around the pan and when it shimmers, about 1 minute, add the onion and cook for 3 minutes, or until softened.

3 Add the garlic and corn and cook for 2 minutes, or until the garlic is fragrant. Add the cream cheese, cumin, and pepper and stir until combined.

4 Add half the spinach and cook for 2 minutes to wilt it, then add the remaining spinach and cook for another 2 minutes to wilt, stirring everything together to combine. Transfer the mixture to a large bowl and stir in three-quarters of the shredded cheese.

5 Wet a clean dish towel and wring it out well, then wrap it around the tortillas and microwave for 2 minutes to steam and soften them.

6 Spread ¾ cup of the creamy green sauce over the bottom of a 9 x 13-inch casserole dish. Fill the tortillas by adding a couple of tablespoons of filling to each, rolling them up, and arranging them seam-side down in the casserole dish. Continue snuggling them in until all the tortillas are in the casserole. Pour the remaining sauce over the top and sprinkle evenly with the remaining shredded cheese.

7 Bake until the cheese is melted and slightly browned and the cream sauce is bubbling, 20 to 25 minutes. Remove from the oven and top with the cilantro. Serve warm, with hot sauce for more spice.

Try making my Charred Green Salsa (page 65) instead of using store-bought!

THE ULTIMATE VEGGIE BURGER

Garth and I love all kinds of food, but like most of you, we understand that we have to find healthy options to balance out our indulgent moments. It's all about moderation. When I started making some vegetarian entrées to mix in with our classic dinners, Garth challenged me to make sure these dishes didn't fall into the "this is good for a healthy recipe" category, but that they would all be really tasty options that we would enjoy eating regularly. I make several different kinds of veggie burgers now, and the ultimate test for me is that they taste great and hold together during cooking. You can pan-fry these burgers in a skillet with a little olive oil, or bake them like I do here. Either way, they're yummy (and also good for you!).

SERVES 8

TY's Special Sauce

½ cup mayonnaise

⅓ cup ketchup

½ to 1 teaspoon hot sauce (I like Tabasco)

¼ teaspoon Worcestershire sauce

Veggie Burgers

2 large sweet potatoes

3 tablespoons olive oil

1 small onion, finely diced

2 garlic cloves, minced

1 teaspoon chili powder

1 (15-ounce) can chickpeas, drained and rinsed

1 (15-ounce) can black beans, drained and rinsed

1 egg, beaten

¼ cup all-purpose flour

1 cup seasoned bread crumbs

1 cup crushed saltine crackers (about ¾ sleeve)

½ cup finely grated Parmesan cheese

1 teaspoon kosher salt

½ teaspoon freshly ground black pepper

8 onion rolls, toasted

Your preferred burger toppings

1 **MAKE THE SAUCE:** In a medium bowl, combine the mayo, ketchup, hot sauce, and Worcestershire; mix well and set aside.

2 **MAKE THE BURGERS:** Preheat the oven to 400°F, with two racks in the middle of the oven. Line a baking sheet with aluminum foil.

3 Set the sweet potatoes on the baking sheet and bake until soft, about 1 hour. Remove from the oven and let them cool. Reduce the oven temperature to 375°F. Line two baking sheets with parchment paper.

4 In a small skillet, heat 1 tablespoon of the olive oil over medium-high heat until shimmering, about 2 minutes. Add the onion and sauté until softened, 3 to 4 minutes. Then stir in the garlic and chili powder and cook for 1 minute more.

5 When cool enough to handle, halve the sweet potatoes, then scoop the flesh into a medium bowl. Add the chickpeas, black beans, and onion mixture and, using a potato masher, mash to break up the beans and combine.

6 Add the egg, flour, bread crumbs, saltines, Parmesan, salt, and pepper. Mix until fully combined. Form the mixture into 8 patties. Divide the patties between the prepared baking sheets and brush both sides with the remaining 2 tablespoons olive oil.

7 Bake for 15 minutes, then flip all the burgers and switch the pans (top and bottom) and rotate them 180 degrees. Bake for 10 to 15 minutes more, until the edges are a light golden brown.

8 Serve the burgers on toasted onion rolls spread with the special sauce. Top with your favorite burger fixings.

SHEET PAN BUDDHA BOWL

A Buddha bowl gets its name for its big round shape resembling Buddha's belly, but I like to think this bowl was named for the balance Buddha inspires! Top the grains of your choice with savory root veggies, sweet pickled beets, and perfectly spicy avocado sauce for a feeling of peace and satisfaction. Roasting all the vegetables together on one sheet pan makes this an easy, stress-free dinner. I top the bowls with roasted salted sunflower seeds, but pepitas are also a great option! Make this bowl your own. We all need a little more nirvana in our lives, don't we?

SERVES 4

2 cups farro, pearled or semipearled

1 large bunch collard greens (12 to 14 leaves)

1 large sweet onion (I like Vidalia)

8 regular-size black tea bags or 4 family-size bags, paper tags removed

Kosher salt and freshly ground black pepper

Olive oil

2½ cups diced (½-inch pieces) butternut squash (14 to 16 ounces)

1 teaspoon chili powder

10 Brussels sprouts, trimmed

2 tablespoons white balsamic vinegar

2 teaspoons honey

½ cup pickled beets

Smoky Avocado Sauce

1 avocado

1 tablespoon plain Greek yogurt

1 canned chipotle chile in adobo

1 tablespoon honey

1½ tablespoons fresh lemon juice (from 1 small lemon)

Kosher salt

1 (15-ounce) can chickpeas, drained and rinsed, for serving

¼ cup roasted, salted sunflower seeds, for garnish

1 Preheat the oven to 400°F. Line a rimmed baking sheet with parchment paper.

2 Rinse and drain the farro, then soak in water for 20 minutes.

3 While the farro soaks, bring 3 quarts water to a boil in a large pot.

4 Stem the collards and cut the leaves into 2- to 3-inch pieces. Cut the onion in half from root to stem, then slice it into ½-inch-wide wedges. Some of the onion wedges will hold together and others will be in pieces—both are fine!

5 Tie the strings of the tea bags together. Drain the farro and add it to the pot of boiling water. Add the tea bags and 1 tablespoon salt. Cook the farro like pasta, stirring occasionally and tasting for doneness, 15 to 25 minutes. Discard the tea bags, drain the farro, and transfer to a medium bowl. Toss with 2 tablespoons olive oil and set aside.

6 In a large bowl, toss the squash with 2 tablespoons olive oil, 2 large pinches of salt, a pinch of pepper, and the chili powder. Arrange the squash on the left side of the prepared baking sheet.

7 Put the onions in the same bowl and drizzle with 2 tablespoons olive oil. Season with a pinch each of salt and pepper. Toss and add to the right side of the baking sheet.

8 Next, combine the collards, 1 tablespoon oil, and a pinch each of salt and pepper in the same bowl and toss the collards to soften them up a bit. Don't add them to the pan—just set aside.

9   Roast the squash and onions on the center rack for 15 minutes, then remove the pan. Keeping them separate, stir the squash and onions and scoot each to the far left and right sides of the pan making an open center space to place the collards on the pan. Spread the collards out in the middle. It will look like a lot, but the collard greens will cook down in the oven.

10 Roast for 15 minutes, then stir once, keeping all the vegetables in their own sections, and rotate the pan. Cook until the squash is tender, the collards are a little crispy, and the onions are roasted and have started to caramelize, about 15 minutes more.

11 Meanwhile, prepare the other fixings. Cut the Brussels sprouts in half, then cut them into fine slaw-like shavings. Transfer to a medium bowl and toss with a pinch each of salt and pepper, the vinegar, 1 tablespoon olive oil, and the honey. Set aside to marinate.

12 Slice the beets into sticks and set aside.

13 **MAKE THE AVOCADO SAUCE**: Scoop the avocado flesh into a blender or small food processor and add the yogurt, chipotle in adobo, honey, lemon juice, ½ teaspoon salt and ¼ cup water. Blend until smooth, about 2 minutes. Set aside.

14 To make the Buddha bowls, divide the farro, vegetables, and chickpeas evenly among four individual serving bowls, then drizzle them with the smoky avocado dressing and top with toasted sunflower seeds.

TRISHA'S TIPS

Cooking the grains in water flavored with black tea adds flavor and color. You can leave this step out and just cook them in salted water, if you prefer.

I like to put all the fixings out in small bowls so everyone can fill and top their Buddha bowls exactly how they like.

Depending on the kind of farro you buy, it could take up to 30 minutes to cook, so hang in there! I usually buy pearled farro. It has no husk and all the bran has been polished away, so it cooks a little faster. Semipearled farro has part of the husk remaining, and requires about 30 minutes to cook.

Quinoa or your favorite kind of rice is a great substitute for farro, if you prefer.

Buddha Bowl

Breads

Bread deserves some love. So many diets tell us that we need to eliminate bread, and I say a big NO to that. I'm not for getting rid of any food group, especially one as tasty and satisfying as this. Julia Child said, "Everything in moderation, including moderation," and I agree wholeheartedly. There are a lot of family ties in this chapter, including Beth's mother-in-law Blanche's sourdough starter bread, my grandma Paulk's sky-high biscuits, and new Yearwood-Brooks family favorites like fresh herbed crackers and skillet cheddar cornbread.

HERBED FOCACCIA BREAD

Beth's friend Leeann is a gifted and generous baker. She always takes extra loaves of this toasted herbed focaccia over to Beth for her family to enjoy. To make this bread for yourself, just remember the dough needs to rise for several hours, so I suggest you start the day before you want to serve the bread and let the dough rise in the fridge overnight. Beth's youngest, Bret, loves this focaccia so much that every time he's home from college, he always asks if Leeann has any extra she needs to get rid of! Both the dough and the baked bread freeze well, and if you ever have leftovers, it makes tasty croutons.

◆

MAKES 1 LARGE LOAF

½ cup olive oil, plus more for topping

2 tablespoons Italian seasoning

½ teaspoon granulated garlic

3 cups all-purpose flour

1 tablespoon kosher salt

2 teaspoons active dry yeast

2 teaspoons honey

1¾ cups warm water

½ cup freshly grated Asiago or Parmesan cheese

1 tablespoon flaky sea salt

1 In a small saucepan, combine the olive oil, Italian seasoning, and garlic and slowly warm over low heat to infuse the oil, stirring occasionally so the herbs don't burn, until fragrant, about 8 minutes. Remove from the heat and let cool to room temperature.

2 In a large bowl, whisk together the flour, salt, and yeast. Add the honey to the warm water and stir to dissolve, then stir the honey mixture into the flour mixture along with ¼ cup of the infused olive oil. Stir together until combined enough to turn out onto a lightly floured work surface. Knead the dough by hand 4 to 6 times until the dough is just formed and sticky.

3 Pour the remaining infused oil into a large bowl (see Tip). Form the dough into a nice ball, then add the dough to the bowl and roll it over to coat with the oil. Cover tightly with plastic wrap and let the dough rise in the refrigerator for at least 8 hours or overnight.

4 The next day, coat a 13 x 18-inch baking sheet with a generous rub of olive oil. Pour the dough into the prepared pan and gently press it out in the pan. Don't worry if it doesn't fill the pan, as it will rise. Cover the pan lightly with plastic wrap and place in a warm spot to rise. The dough will rise and spread in the pan, depending on the warmth of your kitchen, 30 to 60 minutes.

5 While the dough rises, preheat the oven to 450°F.

6 Once the dough is ready, use your fingertips to make gentle dimples in the dough. Then brush with ¼ cup olive oil so the dough is coated and some dimples are little bowls of oil.

7 Sprinkle the Asiago and flaky salt on top and bake for 15 to 20 minutes, until the cheese is melted and golden brown. Let cool on a wire rack. Store in an airtight container for up to two weeks.

Make sure the bowl you put the dough in is big enough for the dough to double in size.

BLANCHE'S SOURDOUGH BREAD & STARTER

One of the positive results of being home during the pandemic was that we all started cooking and baking more. Sourdough starters have become the rage again, and I couldn't be happier. A lot of great bread gets made, and the sharing of the starter creates that sense of community that we've all been missing in our lives. Embrace the good! Beth's kids have sweet memories of mornings at their "Mamaw" Blanche's house that began with warm sourdough bread for breakfast. She kept the starter in a quart jar in her refrigerator, and made fresh bread on the regular. Besides being amazing right out of the oven, the bread is delicious toasted, with a little butter or your favorite jam.

MAKES 3 LOAVES

6 cups bread flour, plus more for dusting

1 (¼-ounce) packet active dry yeast (2¼ teaspoons)

1 tablespoon kosher salt

½ cup corn oil, plus more for greasing

1½ cups warm water

1 cup Blanche's Starter (recipe follows)

2 tablespoons butter, melted

Nonstick cooking spray

1   In a large bowl, combine the flour, yeast, and salt. Make a well in the center and add the oil, water, starter, and melted butter to the well. Stir with a wooden spoon to make a stiff, shaggy dough.

2   Tip the dough out onto a floured work surface and knead it 15 to 20 times, bringing it together into a smooth ball.

3   Grease the bowl you used for the dough with 3 tablespoons oil. Put the dough in the bowl and turn to coat with the oil, then cover loosely with a tent of plastic wrap. Leave on the counter to rise overnight.

4   The next morning, spray three 9 x 5-inch loaf pans with cooking spray.

5   The dough should have tripled in size. Punch down the dough and knead it on a floured surface 7 to 10 times. Divide the dough into 3 equal parts, then knead each 12 to 15 times to bring together into 3 balls. Fold the end of each loaf into the center on all sides 8 to 10 times, forming into 7-inch-long logs. Fit each log into one of the greased loaf pans and brush the dough with oil. Cover the pans loosely with plastic wrap and let rise for 3½ to 5 hours, until they have more than doubled in size.

6   Preheat the oven to 350°F, with a rack in the lower third.

7   Place all 3 loaves on the lower rack, evenly spaced apart. Bake for 40 to 45 minutes, rotating after 30 minutes, until the bread is golden brown and domed.

8   Turn one loaf out immediately onto a wire rack. Tap it on the bottom with your knuckles. The loaf should sound hollow and the bottom should be golden brown. If so, turn out the remaining loaves onto the rack to cool. If not, return the loaves to the oven for 5 minutes more, then repeat the process. Let cool completely on the rack.

See photo page 187

Blanche's Starter

3 (¼-ounce) packets active dry yeast (6¾ teaspoons)

1½ cups warm water, plus 1 cup more for each feeding

⅔ cup sugar, plus ¾ cup more for each feeding

3 tablespoons instant potato flakes, plus 3 tablespoons more for each feeding

In a sterilized quart-size glass jar, dissolve the yeast in ½ cup of the warm water. Add the remaining 1 cup warm water, ⅔ cup sugar, and 3 tablespoons potato flakes. Stir well with a wooden spoon and cover loosely with a lid or a clean dish towel. The mixture should bubble and foam vigorously over the next 30 minutes. Let the mixture stand at room temperature for 8 hours, then refrigerate for 2 to 5 days. It will have bubbles rising in it like a glass of soda.

Feed the starter by adding 1 cup warm water, ¾ cup sugar, and 3 tablespoons potato flakes and stir gently with a clean wooden spoon. Return the starter to the refrigerator to ferment for 8 hours or overnight before using.

Stir the starter well, as it will have settled. Remove 1 cup of the starter to make the bread. Feed the remaining starter 1 cup warm water, ¾ cup sugar, and 3 tablespoons potato flakes and return the jar to the refrigerator.

To maintain the starter, feed it 1 cup warm water, ¾ cup sugar, and 3 tablespoons potato flakes every 3 to 5 days, using or discarding 1 cup every time so it always has the same balance of ingredients.

TRISHA'S TIPS If the starter doesn't bubble when you first make it, discard it and start again! Check to make sure your yeast is not out of date.

The starter will be most bubbly and active when you first make it, but performs better in later feedings than the first.

Timeline

MORNING OF DAY 1: Begin the starter. Let it sit at room temperature.

END OF DAY 1: Put the starter in the refrigerator.

MORNING OF DAY 4: Feed the starter and return to the refrigerator.

EVENING OF DAY 4: Use 1 cup of the starter to make bread; feed the remaining starter and return it to the refrigerator.

(The bread proofs overnight, so in the morning you can make into loaves.)

EVENING OF DAY 9: Use 1 cup of the starter to make bread; feed the remaining starter and return it to the refrigerator.

You'll get in a cycle of using and feeding it every five days.

Blanche Bernard and Ashley, 1991

HOT HONEY CORNBREAD

This delicious bread is for those discerning cornbread lovers who want some real heat. The type of pepper you choose will determine the amount of heat, and if you leave the seeds in like I do, it's even hotter. I eat this cornbread warm, right out of the oven, with a drizzle of the hot honey that creates the sweet heat I love. Leftover cornbread is great crumbled up and served underneath a bed of my Instant Pot Collard Greens (page 103).

◆

SERVES 4 TO 6

2 cups yellow cornmeal

1 cup all-purpose flour

1 tablespoon baking powder

Kosher salt

1 hot chile pepper (such as serrano, Fresno, or jalapeño), thinly sliced

1 cup (2 sticks) butter, at room temperature

2 cups buttermilk

2 large eggs, lightly beaten

¾ cup honey

½ teaspoon cayenne pepper

1 Preheat the oven to 400°F. Put a 10-inch cast-iron skillet in the oven to preheat.

2 In a large bowl, whisk together the cornmeal, flour, baking powder, and 2 teaspoons salt. Add the sliced chile and toss to coat.

3 Remove the skillet from the oven and add ½ cup (1 stick) of the butter to the skillet to melt. Pour the melted butter into a large bowl. Add the buttermilk, eggs, and ½ cup of the honey and whisk together. Stir the buttermilk mixture into the dry mixture, then pour the batter into the hot skillet.

4 Bake until golden brown on top, 35 to 40 minutes. Remove from the oven and let cool.

5 While the cornbread is cooling, in a small bowl, mix the remaining ½ cup (1 stick) butter, ¼ cup honey, the cayenne, and a pinch of salt until completely combined.

6 Serve the cornbread with the hot honey drizzled over the top.

HERBED CRACKERS

I love to create charcuterie boards (just a fancy name for a meat-and-cheese board, really!). I combine my favorite cold meats and cheeses with olives, sweet Peppadew peppers, Spanish almonds, spicy red pepper jelly, you name it. I usually toss in several varieties of breads and crackers. I LOVE making these homemade herbed crackers to go along with everything else on the board. They taste amazing, and your guests will be so impressed. See how many of your friends can even pronounce "charcuterie"! Serve these crackers with your favorite cheeses and my Spicy Red Pepper Jelly (page 205).

MAKES 24 TO 30 CRACKERS

1½ cups all-purpose flour

½ cup whole wheat flour

2 tablespoons butter, at room temperature

1 teaspoon kosher salt, plus more as needed

3 tablespoons grated onion

1½ tablespoons fresh thyme

1½ tablespoons minced fresh chives

½ cup milk

1 egg white, whisked

1 tablespoon sesame seeds

1 Preheat the oven to 450°F.

2 In the bowl of a stand mixer fitted with the paddle attachment, combine the all-purpose and whole wheat flours, butter, and salt and mix on medium-low speed until the mixture resembles a coarse meal. Add the onion, thyme, chives, and milk and mix until just combined. Do not overwork the dough.

3 Roll out the dough into an ⅛-inch-thick rectangle on a lightly floured piece of parchment paper. Brush the top with the egg white and sprinkle with the sesame seeds and additional salt.

4 Transfer the dough on the parchment to a baking sheet and cut it into 2 x 3-inch rectangles. Bake until golden, 10 to 12 minutes. Let cool completely. Store in a sealed plastic bag at room temperature for up to 2 weeks.

GRANDMA'S SKY-HIGH BISCUITS

My Grandma Lizzie used to make biscuits to go along with every meal. Most often, she made a quick buttermilk biscuit, but sometimes for Sunday dinner she made these high-rise yeasted biscuits. I remember them fondly. My grandaddy called them cathead biscuits because he said they were as big as a cat's head! At the end of the meal he would poke a hole in the side of this fluffy biscuit and pour in some honey or maple syrup for his dessert. The folding and refolding of the dough gives them all those wonderful layers. You'll love how light and tall these biscuits are!

MAKES 12 BISCUITS

5 cups all-purpose flour, plus more as needed

1½ teaspoons baking powder

1 teaspoon baking soda

Kosher salt

5 tablespoons sugar

¼ cup warm water (90° to 110°F)

2 (¼-ounce) packets active dry yeast (4½ teaspoons)

1 cup (2 sticks) butter, cut into small cubes and chilled, plus more for greasing and 4 tablespoons (½ stick), melted

2 cups buttermilk

1 Preheat the oven to 425°F.

2 In a large bowl, whisk together the flour, baking powder, baking soda, 1½ teaspoons salt, and 3 tablespoons of the sugar.

3 In a small bowl, combine the warm water, yeast, and remaining 2 tablespoons sugar. Stir until the yeast has dissolved. Let stand until bubbles appear, 2 to 3 minutes.

4 Using your hands, mix the 1 cup (2 sticks) cold butter into the flour, breaking the butter into small pebbles, until the mixture resembles coarse meal. Make a well in the center and add the buttermilk and the yeast mixture. Gently fold the flour into the wet ingredients. Keep mixing until a ball starts to form, then flour your hands and gently knead in the bowl 12 to 15 times, to create a smooth dough. If the mixture is too sticky to easily knead, sprinkle 2 to 3 tablespoons of flour over the top as you knead. Cover with a clean dish towel or plastic wrap and let rise in a warm place for about 1 hour.

5 Transfer the dough to a well-floured work surface. Flour your hands and press the dough out to 2 inches thick. Fold the dough in half, press it out again to 2 inches thick, then fold and press again into a 2-inch-thick square slab.

6 Grease a 10-inch cast-iron skillet with butter. Cut the dough into 12 equal squares and tuck the corners under to make each biscuit into a ball, trying not to mash down too much, then add to the greased skillet. The biscuits will be snug and puff up together when they bake. Brush the tops of the biscuits with melted butter and sprinkle each with a pinch of salt.

7 Bake for 24 to 28 minutes, until golden brown and a toothpick inserted between the center biscuits comes out clean. Brush again with melted butter and serve warm.

My grandparents, Winnes and Lizzie Paulk, 1960

SKILLET CHEDDAR CORNBREAD

Cornbread is as much a part of being Southern as a buttered biscuit. When I'm asked to choose one or the other for my bread option on a menu, it's an almost impossible choice! Adding in the goodness of extra-sharp cheddar and Parmesan cheeses makes for a lighter, fluffier cornbread. As it bakes, the edges and bottom of the cornbread will get dark brown, bathed in caramelized butter and cheese. Sometimes I make this special bread in small, personalized skillets so everybody gets their own pan!

SERVES 6 TO 8

10 tablespoons (1¼ sticks) butter, cut into 1-inch slabs

2 cups self-rising buttermilk cornmeal mix (see Tip)

2 tablespoons sugar

½ teaspoon freshly ground black pepper

8 ounces extra-sharp cheddar cheese, finely grated

½ cup grated Parmesan cheese

1½ cups milk

2 large eggs, lightly beaten

1 Preheat the oven to 425°F, with a rack set in the middle.

2 In an 8-inch cast-iron skillet, melt the butter over medium heat, swirling the pan to coat the sides. Once the butter has melted, remove the pan from the heat and let cool for 1 to 2 minutes.

3 Meanwhile, in a large bowl, stir together the cornmeal mix, sugar, and pepper to combine. Add the cheddar and Parmesan and toss to evenly disperse them throughout the dry mixture. Add the melted butter, leaving a good slick of butter in the skillet. Add the milk and stir to just combine. Add the eggs and stir to form a thick batter.

4 The skillet should still be a little warm and coated with butter, so use oven mitts when handling. Pour the cornbread batter into the skillet and place on the center rack of the oven. Bake for 25 to 28 minutes, until warm, golden brown, and a toothpick inserted into the middle of the cornbread comes out clean. Let the cornbread cool for 5 to 10 minutes before serving.

TRISHA'S TIPS

If you don't have self-rising buttermilk cornmeal mix, make your own by mixing 1¾ cups finely ground cornmeal, 6 tablespoons all-purpose flour, 2 tablespoons baking powder, and ½ teaspoon kosher salt. Measure out 2 cups of the mixture.

Stick with extra-sharp cheddar cheese (grate it yourself instead of buying it pre-grated). Extra sharp cheddar is drier than mild or medium cheddar. More moisture in the other cheeses will cause you to lose the light, fluffy texture of this cornbread, as will pre-grated cheese.

JALAPEÑO HUSH PUPPIES

As a kid, one of Beth's and my favorite summertime activities was when Daddy spent the day with us fishing on our small pond in Monticello, Georgia. He dug out that pond, fed by a spring, using his small farm tractor and stocked it with catfish. Our dad did all the work, baiting our hooks and taking any fish that we happened to catch off the line. I don't think he minded, though, because he got a big kick out of seeing his little girls giggling and squealing every time the red-and-white bobber moved in the water! Mama always fried up our catch with hush puppies on the side. I added the jalapeño and creamed corn for a little something extra. Dip the hush puppies in the hot dipping sauce, and serve alongside my Cornflake-Fried Catfish (page 156).

SERVES 8 TO 10

Vegetable oil, for frying (about 1½ quarts)

1½ cups self-rising buttermilk cornmeal mix (see Tip)

1 cup self-rising flour

½ onion, finely chopped

1 (7-ounce) can diced jalapeños, drained, or 6 fresh jalapeños, seeded and diced

1 (15-ounce) can cream-style corn

2 large eggs, lightly beaten

Kosher salt

Sweet Hot Dipping Sauce

Makes about ¾ cup

½ cup mayonnaise

2 tablespoons sour cream

2 tablespoons sweet pickle relish

1 tablespoon apple cider vinegar

1 teaspoon hot paprika

½ teaspoon sugar

½ teaspoon kosher salt

1 Fill a Dutch oven with about 1¼ inches of oil. Clip a deep-fry thermometer to its side and heat the oil over medium heat to 350°F. Preheat the oven to 200°F.

2 In a large bowl, combine the cornmeal mix, flour, onion, jalapeños, corn, and eggs and stir until blended. Let stand for 5 minutes.

3 Working in batches, drop the batter by teaspoonfuls into the hot oil. Don't overcrowd the pot. Leave room for the hush puppies to be turned. Cook, turning, until golden brown, about 1½ minutes each side. Remove from the oil with a slotted spoon and drain on paper towels. Sprinkle the hush puppies with salt while still hot. Transfer to a baking sheet and keep warm in the oven while you fry the remaining batter.

4 **MAKE THE DIPPING SAUCE:** In a small bowl, mix together the mayonnaise, sour cream, relish, vinegar, paprika, sugar, and salt.

5 Serve the hush puppies with the dipping sauce alongside.

If you don't have self-rising buttermilk cornmeal mix, make your own by mixing 1¾ cups finely ground cornmeal, 6 tablespoons all-purpose flour, 2 tablespoons baking powder, and ½ teaspoon kosher salt. Measure out 1½ cups of the mixture.

Preserves, Pickles, Sauces & Spreads

One of the biggest lessons I learned from my mom
and dad about cooking was to not be afraid to try everything.
Even if you fail, you learn something! In the past, a chapter
full of things that might need canning or lots of processing
would have scared me, but I promise you that these sauces and
spreads are easy to make. The only thing extra some of these treats
take is time. The next time someone offers you an overabundance of
fruits like peaches or pears, you'll know what to do with them! And
once you see how easy it is to make barbecue sauce yourself,
I'm pretty sure you won't go back to store-bought.

CHOCOLATE GRAVY

Tina was my roommate at Belmont College in Nashville back in the mid-'80s. Her parents owned and ran a small dairy farm in Pontotoc, Mississippi (they still do!). When I would go home with Tina for a weekend away from school, her folks, Paul Wayne and Avis, would wake us up for breakfast. The catch was, breakfast for them was around four a.m., because they started their milking early and breakfast was only gonna be served once! Tina's daddy would holler at us to wake up, and we'd smell bacon frying, taters cooking, and the sweet chocolate gravy Tina's mama was making for homemade biscuits. I had never had chocolate gravy before, and I quickly learned what all the fuss was about. After our bellies were full, Tina's folks would let us go back to sleep while they started their daily milking routine. Tina and I have a lot in common, from our Southern roots to our family histories of dairy farming to the love of cooking we got from our parents.

1 cup sugar

3½ tablespoons unsweetened cocoa powder

3 tablespoons self-rising flour

1½ cups milk

1 tablespoon butter

1 In a medium bowl, whisk together the sugar, cocoa powder, and flour until there are no lumps. Add the milk and whisk to combine.

2 In a large sauté pan, melt the butter over medium heat. Add the chocolate milk mixture and cook, stirring continuously, until it begins to thicken slightly, 3 to 4 minutes.

3 Reduce the heat to low and cook, stirring continuously, until the sauce thickens to a gravy consistency, 4 to 5 minutes more. Turn off the heat. The gravy will continue to thicken as it stands. Store any leftovers in an airtight container in the refrigerator for up to a week.

TRISHA's TIP

This gravy is great drizzled over hot buttered biscuits, fresh fruit, or ice cream.

SWEET TEA QUICK PICKLES

There are so many different methods of pickling and just as many varieties of flavor and heat. I love them all. This super-easy quick pickle satisfies with the heat of the banana pepper brine, and the hint of sweet from the tea and honey. I keep a gallon of sweet tea in my fridge at all times, like all good Southerners do, but if you don't, you can pick up a small bottle of premade sweet tea at the grocery store. I store these pickles in the refrigerator in a big mason jar.

◆

MAKES 3 CUPS

¾ cup brewed sweet tea

½ cup distilled white vinegar

2 tablespoons honey

1 tablespoon dried chives

1 teaspoon celery seeds

1 teaspoon kosher salt

Brine from 1 (16-ounce) jar hot banana peppers

6 ounces fresh green beans, trimmed

3 mini cucumbers

1   In a saucepan, combine in the sweet tea, vinegar, honey, chives, celery seeds, salt, and brine from the banana peppers (reserve the banana peppers, refrigerated, for another use). Heat over medium-high heat until just boiling and the honey has dissolved, about 4 minutes.

2   Place the green beans in a heatproof dish or container. Slice the mini cucumbers into 8 spears each and add to the container with the green beans. Pour the hot brine over the vegetables and set aside to cool completely, at least 20 minutes before serving or storing. Store in an airtight container in the refrigerator for up to 3 weeks.

Mini cucumbers are sometimes called pickling or Kirby cucumbers. They're about half the size of a regular cucumber, and perfect for these pickles.

After draining the brine from your jar of banana peppers, refill it with distilled white vinegar and return it to your fridge to sit for a couple of days. It will refresh the banana peppers.

SPICY RED PEPPER JELLY

I inherited my love of spicy things from my mama, Gwen. She would always put a little pepper jelly on her vegetables at dinner, especially when she made black-eyed peas. The red pepper flakes give this jelly a kick, and the sweetness of the preserves is a nod to Mama's favorite fruit: the apricot! I love this jelly smeared on Grandma's Sky-High Biscuits (page 194).

MAKES 1 CUP

1 cup apricot preserves

1 red bell pepper, chopped

2 teaspoons red pepper flakes

¼ cup distilled white vinegar

¼ teaspoon kosher salt

In a blender, combine the preserves, bell pepper, red pepper flakes, vinegar, and salt. Puree until smooth. Transfer the mixture to a small saucepan and bring to a brisk simmer over medium heat. Cook, stirring often, until thickened and syrupy, about 10 minutes. Transfer to a jar and let cool completely. Store in the refrigerator for up to 1 week.

The Yearwood women, circa 1980

BACON ONION JAM

You already know I'm obsessed with bacon, so you won't be surprised to find that I look for any and every way to use it in my recipes. This jam is decadent. It's sweet and salty at the same time. It's always good on a homemade biscuit, or served alongside any meal. I have added this bacon onion jam to my Thanksgiving repertoire, serving it over the top of turkey slices. I make enough for guests to take a jar home with them. It's *that* good!

MAKES 1 CUP

½ pound thick-cut bacon, cut into large chunks

1 large red onion, diced

1 teaspoon kosher salt

2 sprigs thyme

⅓ cup packed light brown sugar

¼ cup strongly brewed coffee

1 tablespoon apple cider vinegar

1   Heat a cast-iron skillet over medium heat. Add the bacon and cook, stirring occasionally, for 10 to 12 minutes, until the bacon is mostly cooked and almost crispy. Drain the bacon fat from the pan into a heatproof container. There will be about ½ cup fat, which can be kept for another use or discarded once cool (see Tip).

2   Return 1 to 2 tablespoons of the bacon fat to the pan and add the onion, salt, and thyme. Cook over medium heat until the onion starts to brown, 7 to 8 minutes.

3   Add the brown sugar and the coffee to the pan. Scrape the browned bits from the bottom of the pan and cook for 20 to 25 minutes, until the bacon and onions reach a thick, syrupy consistency. Stir in the vinegar. Remove from the heat and discard the thyme stems.

4   Use immediately or store in an airtight container in the refrigerator for up to 1 week.

TRISHA'S TIP

Never pour hot bacon fat down your kitchen sink drain. Tear off a piece of aluminum foil, make a well in the center using a bowl or your fist, and pour the drippings into the well. Seal the foil and discard in the trash. Another way to dispose of bacon drippings is to let them cool completely in the pan until solid, then wipe the pan clean using paper towels and discard in the trash.

PEAR RELISH

In the Yearwood house of my childhood, fresh pears meant fall had arrived. Monticello friends always shared the bounty of their pear crops—and I'm talking *bounty*! We canned quarts and quarts of pears. This relish brings back all those canning memories and adds the fragrance of fall—cinnamon, nutmeg, and cloves. Make this relish and you won't have to wait for the leaves to change to enjoy the sweet taste of fall all year long!

MAKES 2 CUPS

2 large Bartlett or Anjou pears

3 tablespoons butter

Pinch of ground cloves

¼ teaspoon ground cinnamon

2 or 3 shavings of nutmeg

¼ teaspoon kosher salt, plus more if needed

Pinch of freshly ground black pepper

¼ cup pure maple syrup

1 tablespoon bourbon (optional)

1 Peel and core the pears, then cut them into roughly ⅓-inch dice. Warm a high-sided medium skillet over medium-high heat and add the butter. Once the butter has melted, stir in the pears and cook for 3 minutes, or until they start to caramelize a little.

2 Sprinkle in the cloves, cinnamon, nutmeg, salt, and pepper, stirring to coat the pears, and cook until the spices are fragrant, about 2 minutes.

3 Add the maple syrup and simmer, stirring continuously, for 3 minutes. If using the bourbon, add it carefully, as the hot syrup may sputter. Cook for 3 to 4 minutes more, until the liquid reduces to a syrup and the pears soften. Taste and add more salt if desired.

4 Enjoy warm as part of a cheese platter.

TRISHA'S TIP You can substitute ⅛ teaspoon ground nutmeg for the fresh shavings if you want, but one thing I've learned on *Trisha's Southern Kitchen* is that for most spices, ground is okay, but fresh nutmeg really is markedly better, so I say go for it!

TRISHA'S SWEET & SMOKY HOT SAUCE

You can always buy your favorite hot sauce at the grocery store, but when you want to really show off for your friends, try this fresh, easy-to-make smoky sauce. Most people use jalapeños to spice up their sauces and spreads, but I love the red Fresno chile for its nice medium heat and subtle smoky flavor. It's perfect in this hot sauce. I sprinkle this sauce over collard greens and cornbread, or into black-eyed peas for smoky heat. The chipotles in adobo add even more smoky, spicy flavor.

◆

MAKES 2 CUPS

2½ cups distilled white vinegar

2 cups sliced carrots

4 Fresno chiles, stemmed and halved

2 canned chipotle chiles in adobo, plus 2 tablespoons adobo sauce from the can

1 In a small saucepan, combine the vinegar, carrots, and Fresno chiles. Bring to a simmer over medium heat and cook until the carrots are tender, 15 to 20 minutes.

2 Remove from the heat and transfer to a blender. Add the chipotles and adobo sauce and puree. Strain through a fine-mesh strainer into a measuring cup, then pour into a bottle. Store in the refrigerator for up to 3 weeks.

TRISHA'S TIP

If you use a high-powered blender like a Vitamix, you don't need to strain the hot sauce.

MUSCADINE JAM

My longtime guitar player and friend Johnny Garcia and his wife, Lory, grow wild muscadines in their backyard garden. Every year they bring me bags of them, in all variety of colors, from green to bronze to deep purples. Muscadines, sometimes called scuppernongs, grew wild on our farm in Georgia, and I loved to eat them. When people ask me what they are, I always say they're grapes on steroids! Their super-sweet flavor, mixed with the tartness of their thicker skins, makes them perfect for this jam. Pulverizing the skins in a heavy-duty blender like a Vitamix ensures smooth, perfect jam every time. Thanks, Johnny!

MAKES 3 PINTS

4 pounds bronze and purple muscadines

½ cup lemon juice

3 cups sugar

6 tablespoons Sure-Jell (classic) fruit pectin

1 Separate the pulp and skins of the muscadines. (The best way to do this is to slice the top of each muscadine and squeeze out the pulp.) Put the skins and 1 cup water in a medium saucepan and bring to a boil. Put the pulp and 1 cup water in a separate medium saucepan and bring to a boil. Reduce the heat to medium and simmer both pots until the pulp starts to break down, 5 to 6 minutes.

2 Mash the pulp using a potato masher to release as much juice from the pulp as possible, then cook for another 5 to 6 minutes. Remove the pulp from the heat and strain out the seeds, pushing the pulp through a fine-mesh sieve or using a food mill. Discard the seeds.

3 Remove the skins from the heat and puree them in a food processor or high-powered blender until completely smooth. Pour the strained pulp and pureed skins into a large Dutch oven or heavy-bottomed pan over medium heat. Add the lemon juice. Whisk in the sugar and pectin. Cook, stirring at regular intervals, for 45 to 60 minutes. Check the jam's ability to set by placing a spoon in the freezer and when cold enough, dipping it into the mixture. If the jam clings to the spoon, it's ready to process.

4 Process using a hot water bath (see page 214).

5 Ladle the jam into clean, hot 8-ounce canning jars, leaving ¼-inch headspace in each jar. Wipe the rims clean with a damp paper towel, then place the lids and bands on the jars. Process in the boiling water bath for 10 minutes. Remove the jars and set on the counter to seal and cool.

6 Store in a cool, dark spot for up to 1 year. Any jars that don't seal during the canning process can be refrigerated and used within 2 weeks.

Muscadine jam

PEACH MUSTARD
BARBECUE SAUCE

I continue to be inspired by my family, even those who have gone on before me. My daddy, Jack, was a great home cook. He cooked barbecue chicken over a large pit every summer for the whole town. Really! The local Kiwanis club sold tickets on the town square for Jack's barbecue, and they always sold out. A Georgia boy through and through, he loved fresh peaches. I imagine that he would totally approve of this sweet, tangy sauce. I make this barbecue sauce every summer when peach season is in full swing. There's nothing like the sweetness of ripe peaches mixed with the bite of mustard and Worcestershire sauce. Serve this sauce with my Dry-Brined Grilled Chicken (page 146) or over your favorite pulled pork.

MAKES 1½ CUPS

½ sweet onion (I like Vidalia), thinly sliced

2 tablespoons vegetable oil

Kosher salt and freshly ground black pepper

2 cups diced ripe peaches (2 to 3 medium)

⅓ cup prepared yellow mustard

1 teaspoon Worcestershire sauce

2 tablespoons molasses

Pinch of cayenne pepper

1 In a medium skillet, combine the onion, oil, and a pinch each of salt and black pepper. Sauté over medium heat until soft and starting to brown, about 6 minutes. Add the peaches and ¼ cup water and sauté until softened, about 7 minutes.

2 Stir in the mustard, Worcestershire, molasses, and cayenne. Bring to a simmer and cook to infuse the flavors, about 3 minutes.

3 Carefully pour the sauce into a blender and puree until smooth, with the lid slightly ajar and a dish towel over the top to protect you from splatter. Store in the refrigerator for up to 3 weeks.

My dad, Jack, BBQ master and scratch golfer, 1990s

Peach Mustard Barbecue Sauce

Trisha's Sweet & Smoky Hot Sauce 208

BETH'S PEACH PRESERVES

By now, everybody knows my sister, Beth, from my books and TV shows. She's my "person"! This year, when she and her husband, John, decided, as empty nesters, to move back to John's native state of Tennessee, I was over-the-moon excited! The prospect of seeing my sister every day is just heaven to me. She and John found a little spot of land near us to build the perfect forever home. The minute we walked onto the land, we both knew it was the right spot. There were big pecan trees just like the ones in the front yard of our childhood home in Monticello, Georgia. We discovered a small peach orchard and got to enjoy the summer's bounty. We gathered so many bushels of peaches that every day we were looking for new ways to use them. You'll find several peach recipes born out of those days in this book! After many incarnations of preserves, this simple, no-pectin combination made us the happiest. It's the perfect amount of sweetness, while keeping the fresh flavor of Georgia peaches (or in this case, Tennessee peaches!) front and center. Serve on toast, or smear on my Herbed Crackers (page 193).

◆

MAKES 4 PINTS

28 to 30 ripe medium peaches

½ cup fresh lemon juice (from about 4 lemons)

2½ to 3½ cups sugar

1 teaspoon ground cinnamon

1 Bring a large pot of water to a boil, then place the peaches in the water 4 to 6 at a time and boil for 1 to 2 minutes. Remove from the water using a slotted spoon or wire spider and immediately submerge in a bowl of ice and water to stop them from cooking. Leave the peaches in the ice water, and then, one at a time, take them out and peel them; the skins should slide off easily.

2 Pit and dice the peeled peaches, then put them in a large heavy-bottomed saucepan or Dutch oven. Add the lemon juice, 2½ cups sugar, and the cinnamon and stir gently to combine. The amount of sugar you need will depend on the sweetness of the peaches, so add sugar to taste. Let the mixture sit at room temperature for 1 hour, allowing the sugar to macerate the fruit.

3 Bring the mixture to a boil over medium-high heat, stirring occasionally, then reduce the heat to low and cook, stirring occasionally and using a potato masher or pastry blender to periodically break up the peaches into smaller pieces, until the mixture has reduced by almost half and thickened, about 3 hours. As the mixture thickens, you will need to stir more often to prevent sticking and scorching.

4 Can the preserves in 8-ounce jars using the hot water bath method (see page 214).

TRISHA'S TIP

If you don't want to blanch and shock the peaches, or if your peaches are super ripe, use a paring knife to peel them.

Hot Water Bath Method for Sealing Canning Jars

Place a wire rack with handles in the bottom of a large, deep pot with a lid. Fill the pot half full with water, place empty glass jars on the rack, and bring the water to a boil. Boil for 5 minutes, then remove the jars, set them on a clean towel on the kitchen counter, and get ready to fill (hot jars filled with hot preserves are less likely to crack). Keep the water boiling.

Fill a small saucepan with enough water to cover the lids and rings and boil for 5 minutes, then remove from the heat.

Pour the preserves into the glass jars, leaving about ¼-inch headspace. Use a damp paper towel to wipe around the top of the jar for a clean seal. Top with a lid and screw a ring onto each jar until finger-tight. Lower the filled jars slowly and carefully into the boiling water. The water should cover the jars by 1 inch. Add more boiling water, if necessary, to reach this level.

Cover the pot and return the water to a boil, then boil the jars for 10 minutes. Carefully remove the jars from the water and set aside to cool. The jar lids will pop and invert as they seal.

When the jars are cool, remove the rings if the preserves are to be stored before use. If any of the jars do not seal, store in the refrigerator and eat within 2 weeks. Sealed jars can be stored in your pantry for up to 1 year.

When you're making preserves, it's sometimes hard to tell when hot, pectin-free preserves are thick enough. A good trick is to put a small dish in the freezer until it's really cold (about 10 minutes will do it!). Take the dish out of the freezer and dollop a small spoonful of the preserves onto the dish, then tilt it to see how quickly the preserves run down the dish. Using a frozen dish allows them to cool quickly, so you'll get an idea of how thick your finished preserves will be!

Sweets

My mama used to say after every meal, "Now I just need a little something sweet!" There are so many options in this chapter, it could have been a whole book. From family traditions like my dad's favorite fried pies and my uncle Wilson's ice cream concoction to my double-stuffed brownies and banana split nachos (yes!), you'll surely find something to suit your sweet fancy.

TRISHA'S TIPS

Change up the colors of this cake to make it your own. It's beautiful in pretty pastels for a child's birthday party . . . rename it Unicorn Cake and call it a day!

If you don't have almond flour, add an extra ¼ cup all-purpose flour.

CAMO CAKE

I might be the only person I know who has a complete camo section in her closet! My love of all things camo started in high school, when my dad insisted I keep his old army jacket in the trunk of my car, just in case it ever broke down and I needed a warm coat. It had a thick lining and a classic army-green exterior. I loved that jacket so much! I share my love of camo with my nephew, Kyle. I made him this cake for his birthday one year. It has such a tasty almond flavor, but it's a real showstopper when you slice it and see all those beautiful camo colors inside. Oh, and I still have my daddy's army jacket in the trunk of my car . . . just in case.

SERVES 8

Cake

Nonstick cooking spray

1½ cups granulated sugar

¾ cup (1½ sticks) unsalted butter, at room temperature

1 (8-ounce) package cream cheese, at room temperature

3 large eggs, at room temperature

1 teaspoon almond extract

½ teaspoon vanilla extract

1¾ cups all-purpose flour

½ cup almond flour

1½ teaspoons baking powder

½ teaspoon kosher salt

½ cup milk

Gel food coloring in neon green, black, leaf green, and dark brown

Maple Cream Sauce

2 ounces (¼ of an 8-ounce package) cream cheese, at room temperature

1 teaspoon maple extract

½ cup confectioners' sugar

1 Preheat the oven to 325°F. Spray an 8 x 4-inch loaf pan with cooking spray and line it with parchment paper, leaving some overhanging parchment on the long sides of the pan.

2 In the bowl of a stand mixer fitted with the paddle attachment, combine the granulated sugar, butter, and cream cheese. Cream on medium speed until the mixture is smooth and fluffy, 4 to 5 minutes. Add the eggs one at a time, beating well after each addition, until incorporated. Add the almond and vanilla extracts and whip until combined.

3 Sift together the all-purpose and almond flours, baking powder, and salt onto a sheet of waxed paper. Add half the flour mixture and half the milk to the batter and beat on low speed until just combined. Add the remainder of the milk and then the flour mixture and beat on low speed until the batter is smooth. Divide the batter equally among four small bowls.

4 Use the gel food coloring to create four colors (one in each of the four bowls): light green (3 drops neon green plus 1 drop black); dark green (3 drops leaf green plus 1 drop black); gray (2 drops black); and dark brown (3 drops dark brown).

5 Use small (2-tablespoon) ice cream scoops to drop dollops of the colored batters in random order into the prepared loaf pan to create a camouflage pattern.

6 Bake for 1 hour 25 minutes, or until a toothpick inserted into the center comes out clean. Let cool completely before removing from the pan.

7 MAKE THE MAPLE CREAM SAUCE: In a small saucepan, combine the cream cheese, maple extract, and 2 tablespoons water and heat over medium heat, stirring, until melted and combined. Remove from the heat, then stir in the confectioners' sugar until it has a nice creamy consistency, then drizzle over the cake before serving.

GRANDMA YEARWOOD'S HUNDRED-DOLLAR CUPCAKES

with Caramel Icing

Most of the Yearwood women's recipes are easy to make with simple ingredients, but I will confess that cooked caramel icing can be tricky. It's so worth it, though! Our grandma Yearwood didn't cook that often. She became a widow at fifty, losing her husband, Bo, before I was born. She worked several jobs, which didn't leave her a lot of time to bake, but she always managed to have something sweet for the grandchildren when we came to visit. She somehow always made the caramel turn out perfectly! I have gotten better at making caramel over the years. It just takes practice to know when that magic window is for spreading the icing, so don't give up! The first time Beth and I made these cupcakes for ourselves, the caramel set beautifully, so we are pretty sure Grandma Yearwood was guiding our steps. Legend has it that hundred-dollar cake got its name from a patron at a Chicago restaurant years ago who paid dearly for the recipe for a version of this rich chocolate cake. With inflation, maybe we should call these thousand-dollar cupcakes!

◆

MAKES 24 CUPCAKES

Cupcakes

2 cups sifted cake flour

1½ teaspoons baking powder

¾ teaspoon kosher salt

½ teaspoon baking soda

4 ounces unsweetened chocolate, chopped

1 cup granulated sugar

1 cup packed light brown sugar

½ cup (1 stick) unsalted butter, at room temperature

2 large eggs, at room temperature

2 teaspoons vanilla extract

1½ cups whole milk, at room temperature

Icing

2 cups granulated sugar

¾ cup buttermilk

½ cup (1 stick) unsalted butter

1 teaspoon baking soda

1 teaspoon vanilla extract

Splash of heavy cream, if needed

1 **MAKE THE CUPCAKES:** Preheat the oven to 350°F. Line two 12-cup muffin tins with cupcake liners.

2 In a medium bowl, whisk together the flour, baking powder, salt, and baking soda.

3 Put the chocolate in a microwave-safe bowl and microwave on high in 30-second intervals, stirring after each, until melted, about 1½ minutes total (or melt it in a double boiler).

4 In the bowl of a stand mixer fitted with the paddle attachment, beat the granulated sugar, brown sugar, and butter until light and fluffy, about 3 minutes. Add the melted chocolate and beat to combine.

5 Add the eggs one at a time, beating well after each addition. Beat in the vanilla. Add the flour mixture in three batches, alternating with the milk, beginning and ending with the flour, and beat on low until just combined.

6 Divide the batter evenly among the prepared muffin tins, filling each cupcake liner with about ¼ cup of the batter. Bake until the cupcakes are domed slightly and a toothpick inserted into the center comes out clean, about 18 minutes. Let cool completely on a wire rack.

Grandma Yearwood,
1970s

7 **MAKE THE ICING RIGHT BEFORE YOU ARE READY TO FROST THE CUPCAKES:** In a medium to large heavy-bottomed saucepan, combine the granulated sugar, buttermilk, butter, baking soda, and vanilla (the liquid will double in volume, so be sure your pan is large enough). Clip a candy thermometer to the side of the pan and bring the mixture to a boil over medium-high heat. Boil until the mixture reaches soft-ball stage (235°F), 10 to 15 minutes. Remove from the heat as it hits the soft-ball stage to avoid overcaramelizing.

8 Working very quickly, but carefully, pour the caramel into the bowl of a stand mixer fitted with the paddle attachment and beat on medium-high speed until cooled to warm, about 5 minutes. Working quickly, spoon about a tablespoon of the caramel icing onto each cupcake. (Caramel hardens a little as it cools. Whip in a splash of cream to loosen it up if needed.) Let stand until set, about 5 minutes, before serving.

Hundred-Dollar Cupcakes

PEAR CHARLOTTE

When Beth and I were little girls, there were only a couple of food shows on TV, and our parents, both excellent home cooks, watched them. My dad loved Justin Wilson, the Cajun chef who made almost everything with a splash of Sauternes (sweet French wine), then drank the rest during the show. His food looked so good, and he was fun to watch! My mom loved Julia Child. Julia became my culinary role model when I found out that she was a home cook, just like me! She made the apple charlotte famous on her TV show, and I remember vividly how when she turned the beautiful dessert out onto a platter, it began to slowly come apart. She just laughed and said it was fine! It would still taste wonderful. She gave me that courage to know that great food doesn't always have to be perfect to be perfect, ya know? I've replaced Julia's apple filling with pears, and it works beautifully. Your guests will never know the crust is brushed white bread! So simple and so good. This rustic dish is a tasty way to use up an overabundance of pears and day-old bread. I've read it was named after Queen Charlotte, wife of George III, but I really have no idea. I just know everyone loves it. And just a note to any home cooks trying this dish for the first time: It "may" slowly fall apart after it comes out of the mold, but it will taste divine! Thank you for the confidence to try everything, Julia!

SERVES 6

4 tablespoons (½ stick) unsalted butter, plus 10 tablespoons (1¼ sticks) at room temperature

6 pounds Bosc and/ or Asian pears, peeled, cored, and chopped (see Tips)

½ teaspoon lemon zest

2 tablespoons fresh lemon juice

¾ cup sugar

1 teaspoon ground cinnamon

½ teaspoon freshly grated nutmeg

½ teaspoon vanilla extract

22 slices white bread, crusts removed

Whipped cream or ice cream, for serving

Special Equipment
7-cup charlotte mold or a flat-bottomed 2-quart ovenproof casserole

1 Preheat the oven to 400°F.

2 In a large saucepan, melt 4 tablespoons (½ stick) of the butter over medium heat. Add the pears, lemon zest, lemon juice, sugar, cinnamon, nutmeg, and vanilla and stir to combine. Cook over medium-low heat, stirring occasionally, until the pears break down and release most of their moisture, and the mixture thickens and has reduced by half to two-thirds, 60 to

80 minutes, depending on how juicy the pears are. You should have about 4 cups cooked filling when it's ready. Remove the pan from the heat and set aside to cool. The filling will continue to thicken as it cools.

3 **TO ASSEMBLE (SEE PAGES 224–225):** Use a rolling pin to flatten the bread slices to half their usual thickness. Arrange 4 of the bread slices in a square shape on a flat surface. Place the charlotte mold (or a 2-quart ovenproof casserole dish) on the bread and trace the edges with a sharp edge. Cut the bread following the traced line and brush both sides with the softened butter. Fit the bread into the bottom of the mold.

4 Cut 11 of the bread slices in half lengthwise. They should be about the same height as the mold. Spread one side of the halved slices with the softened butter and place them with their butter side against the inside of the mold, overlapping them like a fan. (The butter helps grease the mold so the charlotte will be easier to remove.)

Recipe Continues

5 Fill the mold with the pear mixture. Place a slice of well-buttered bread in the center of the mold on top of pear mixture. Cut the remaining 6 slices of bread into triangles, brush with the softened butter, and fan the pieces over the top (like a pinwheel), with the shorter side of the triangle against the outside edge of the mold. Press them down and tuck in the corners as much as possible to fit into the top of the mold.

6 Bake until golden brown, about 30 minutes. Let cool in the mold for 20 to 25 minutes. Run a knife around the inside of the mold to loosen the charlotte, then invert a plate over the top of the mold and, holding the mold and plate together, flip to invert the charlotte onto the plate. Lift the mold off the charlotte gently using the handles of the mold. Serve warm, with whipped cream or ice cream.

If you can find Asian pears, they add a nice blend of flavor and texture with the Bosc pears. You can also use just-ripe Bartlett pears in this charlotte. They are still a little tart and slightly gritty, but sweet at the same time.

This recipe calls for freshly grated nutmeg. You can substitute ground nutmeg, but of all the spices, I highly recommend going the extra mile and grating nutmeg fresh. You really can taste the difference.

WILD MUSCADINE PIE

with Peanut Butter Sauce

Beth and I have enjoyed going through our mom's shoebox full of recipes over the years. So many of these little gems were handwritten on the backs of napkins in our mom's perfect penmanship, or on faded pages in our Grandma Paulk's elegant soft cursive. The memories come flooding back every time we sift through these treasures. We were surprised to find a recipe for scuppernong pie that we couldn't recall ever tasting, so Beth and I made it our mission to try it out. This pie does not disappoint. Muscadines are dark purple wild grapes that have an intense sweet flavor. You'll sometimes hear them called scuppernongs, which is just the lighter bronze or greener variety. (Think green and red grapes on steroids!) I use a mix of all colors and varieties for this pie. The skins are thicker than regular grapes; Cooking them down to soften a little is the key. I describe the flavor of this pie as the most scrumptious grape jelly you've ever tasted. That's why I decided to pair it with a peanut butter drizzle. It just felt like the right thing to do! It's like a PB&J pie!

SERVES 8 TO 10

Pie

6 cups (about 2¼ pounds) black and bronze muscadines

2 cups sugar

¼ teaspoon baking soda

¼ cup cornstarch

4 tablespoons (½ stick) margarine

1 box (2 crusts) refrigerated pie crusts (I like Pillsbury)

1 egg, beaten

Peanut Butter Sauce

Makes 1¼ cups

½ cup natural salted smooth peanut butter (blend well before measuring)

½ cup sweetened condensed milk

1 teaspoon vanilla extract

1 Preheat the oven to 350°F.

2 **MAKE THE PIE:** Separate the pulp and skins of the muscadines. (The best way to do this is to slice the top of each muscadine and squeeze out the pulp.) Put the skins and ½ cup water in a medium saucepan and bring to a boil. Put the pulp in a small saucepan and bring to a boil.

3 Add the sugar to the pot with the skins (do not add sugar to the pulp). Reduce the heat to medium-low and simmer both pots until the pulp starts to break down, 5 to 6 minutes.

4 Mash the pulp using a potato masher to release as much juice from the pulp as possible, then cook for another 5 to 6 minutes.

5 Remove the skins from the heat and puree them in a high-powered blender until completely smooth, then return them to the saucepan. Remove the pulp from the heat and strain it using a food mill or fine-mesh strainer into the pan with the skins, separating the seeds from the pulp. Discard the seeds.

6 Add the baking soda to the mixture. It may turn green and foam up, depending on how purple the mixture is. Don't worry! Just continue to stir and bring to a simmer.

Recipe Continues

7   In a small bowl, combine ¼ cup water and the cornstarch. Mix until there are no lumps. Add the cornstarch slurry to the muscadine mixture and stir, then bring to a boil. Add the margarine and stir until melted. Remove from the heat.

8   Roll out one of the pie crusts and transfer it to a 9-inch pie pan. Pour the filling into the uncooked crust. Roll out the second crust and set it on top of the pie. Pinch the dough together all the way around the pie to seal the edges. Cut vents in the top crust in several places. Brush with the beaten egg using a pastry brush. Bake until the crust has browned, 45 to 50 minutes.

9   **MAKE THE PEANUT BUTTER SAUCE**: Meanwhile, in a small saucepan, combine the peanut butter, condensed milk, and 5 tablespoons water and cook over low heat, stirring, until smooth. Turn off the heat and stir in the vanilla.

10 Drizzle the peanut butter sauce over the baked muscadine pie. Store leftover pie in an airtight container in the fridge for up to 2 weeks (if it lasts that long!).

A food mill is a great kitchen tool, and can be used to separate seeds any time you're seeding fruits like berries, grapes, or tomatoes. If you don't have one, a fine-mesh strainer will work. Press on the pulp with a spatula, pushing as much juice through the strainer as possible.

You don't have to puree the skins. If you add them whole, you'll have nice bites of chewy grape skins mixed in with the smooth jelly of the pie. I love this pie either way!

The peanut butter sauce is also great served over ice cream. I use natural peanut butter here, but regular is fine.

LEMON PECAN SLAB PIE

This slab pie was born out of a basic pecan pie recipe I got from my Monticello friend Miss Betty Maxwell years ago. She told me the secret to this pie was to whisk the filling ingredients by hand, not to whip them in a mixer, or it will get too thin and never set in the crust. I added lemon juice and zest to my pecan pie because I love the combination of flavors. I serve this slab pie at Thanksgiving. It serves more folks and is much easier to cut into squares and serve at room temperature. It makes a lot of pie for a big gathering.

SERVES 18 TO 20

Nonstick cooking spray

2 boxes (2-count each) refrigerated pie crusts (I like Pillsbury)

2 cups packed dark brown sugar

1 cup granulated sugar

4 large eggs

¼ cup all-purpose flour

¼ cup milk

1 cup (2 sticks) unsalted butter, melted

1 tablespoon vanilla extract

1 heaping tablespoon lemon zest

¼ cup plus 2 tablespoons fresh lemon juice

2 cups chopped pecans, plus 3 cups pecan halves

1 Preheat the oven to 325°F. Spray a 17 x 12-inch baking sheet with cooking spray.

2 Unroll the pie crusts and place them on the baking sheet. Line them up so they meet in the center of the baking sheet and overlap a bit. Trim the dough to form a straight seam in the center of the baking sheet and pinch the seam together. Crimp the dough around the edges of the baking sheet and cut off any excess dough.

3 In a large bowl, whisk together the brown sugar, granulated sugar, and eggs until incorporated. Whisk the flour into the milk until dissolved, then stir into the dry mixture, along with the butter, vanilla, lemon zest, lemon juice, and chopped pecans until combined. Pour the mixture into the unbaked pie shell. Arrange the pecan halves on top of the pie. Bake until the crust is golden brown and the filling is set but still a little loose in the center (it will set as it cools), about 55 minutes. Cut into squares and serve warm or at room temperature.

SUMMER BERRY SLAB PIE

My easy summer go-to pie is this colorful slab pie with all my favorite fresh berries. It is a beautiful presentation, and however you choose to do the simple cutout dough pieces will make it your own. You can skip that step and just top with the second crust, but I recommend getting creative and seeing what you come up with. Every time I make this pie, I use different shapes and sizes of cookie cutters to make it unique. The raspberries are too delicate to mix in with the blackberries and blueberries, so I add them at the end to maintain their shape.

SERVES 12 TO 16

18 ounces blackberries

18 ounces blueberries

1 cup plus 1 tablespoon Demerara sugar or raw sugar (see Tips)

1 teaspoon kosher salt

1 tablespoon grated fresh ginger

Zest of 1 lemon

5 tablespoons cornstarch

3 boxes (2-count each) refrigerated pie crusts (I like Pillsbury)

1 large egg

18 ounces raspberries

2 tablespoons butter, cut into ½-inch cubes

Special Equipment
The two smallest rounded flower cookie cutters in a stackable set (mine were 1¾ inches and 2¼ inches)

1 In a large bowl, combine the blackberries, blueberries, 1 cup sugar, salt, ginger, lemon zest, and cornstarch. Stir well to combine and let the mixture macerate, or meld together, in the bowl for 20 minutes while you prepare the dough.

2 Preheat the oven to 425°F, with a rack in the lower third.

3 On a lightly floured surface, unroll 3 rounds of the pie dough and stack into a pile. Roll out into a 14 x 19-inch rectangle. Place the dough rectangle on a 13 x 18-inch rimmed baking sheet. There should be a slight overhang on all four sides. Trim any excess and press the dough so it just rolls over the edge of the baking sheet. Poke the dough a few times with a fork and bake until it is barely brown, 5 to 6 minutes. Remove from the oven and let cool. Reduce the oven temperature to 400°F. Line a baking sheet with parchment paper.

4 Unroll and stack the remaining 3 rounds of pie dough. Roll out into a 14 x 19-inch rectangle. Place the dough rectangle on the prepared baking sheet. This will be the top crust of the pie.

5 Dip the larger flower cookie cutter in a little flour and cut 7 or 8 evenly spaced pieces from the unbaked dough rectangle, leaving a 2-inch border and saving the cutouts on a lightly flour-dusted plate. Repeat with the smaller flower cutter, saving the smaller cutouts as well. Place the pie top and the cutouts in the refrigerator to chill for 20 minutes.

6 To assemble the pie, in a small bowl, whisk together the egg and 1 teaspoon water to make an egg wash.

7 Pour the blueberry-blackberry mixture into the partially baked crust bottom, spreading it evenly, then add the raspberries evenly into the filling. Dot the cubes of butter evenly over the filling. Brush a little egg wash over the rimmed edge of the bottom crust.

8 Remove the top crust and cutouts from the fridge. Use a rolling pin to lift and roll the dough off the baking sheet and lay it over the pie. Pinch the edges of the pie together all the way around.

9 Brush the top of the crust with egg wash, then decorate with the cutout flowers and brush their tops with egg wash. Sprinkle all over with the remaining 1 tablespoon Demerara sugar.

Recipe Continues

10 Bake for 30 to 35 minutes, until the filling is bubbling and the crust is golden brown. Let cool completely, at least 40 minutes, before slicing.

Demerara sugar is a type of large-grain cane sugar with a pale amber color. You can substitute brown sugar, or any kind of large-crystal raw sugar.

Partially baking, or parbaking, the bottom crust before adding the filling keeps the crust from becoming soggy.

BLUEBERRY PIE BARS

Garth started his first-ever stadium tour in 2019, selling out huge football fields all over the country. Watching him make a crowd of anywhere from sixty to one hundred thousand people feel like an intimate family reunion is a sight to behold, and it's been so fun to bring everybody together. Concertgoers come early, stay all day, and tailgate like they do for football games, so Garth encouraged me to host my own Trisha's Tailgate at these concerts. Before every show, we put up a huge tent and provide food, drinks, and games, giving folks a place to hang out before the big show. I have loved every minute of these events. I change up the food so it's a little different at every party. We made these blueberry pie bars for the first tailgate we hosted at Notre Dame, and they were such a big hit, we've included them in every Trisha's Tailgate since.

◆

MAKES 9 BARS

Crust

Nonstick cooking spray

½ cup (1 stick) unsalted butter, chilled

¾ cup sugar

1½ cups all-purpose flour

½ teaspoon ground cinnamon

Pinch of kosher salt

Filling

1 large egg

½ heaping cup sour cream

⅓ cup sugar

2 tablespoons fresh lemon juice

1 tablespoon all-purpose flour

4 teaspoons cornstarch

2 teaspoons vanilla extract

½ teaspoon ground cinnamon

2 cups blueberries

1 **MAKE THE CRUST:** Preheat the oven to 350°F. Spray an 8-inch square baking pan with cooking spray. Line the pan with parchment paper so that it hangs over on two sides. Spray the parchment.

2 In a food processor, combine the butter, sugar, flour, cinnamon, and salt. Process until the mixture starts to come together and clump, about 1 minute. Transfer ¾ cup of the mixture to a small bowl and set aside. Press the remaining crust mixture evenly onto the bottom of the prepared pan. Set aside.

3 **MAKE THE FILLING:** In a medium bowl, whisk together the egg, sour cream, sugar, lemon juice, flour, cornstarch, vanilla, and cinnamon until smooth. Mix in 1 cup of the blueberries. Pour the filling over the crust, shaking the pan gently to settle the custard and berries. Pour the remaining 1 cup blueberries over the top, spreading them evenly.

4 Take the reserved crust mixture and sprinkle it over the berries, squeezing the mixture in your hands to encourage large clumps.

5 Bake for 1 hour, or until lightly golden brown. Let cool completely in the pan, then transfer the bars from the pan to a cutting board and cut into 9 pieces. Refrigerate until ready to serve.

PEANUT BUTTER & ROASTED BANANA PUDDING

My daddy's favorite dessert was banana pudding. He never had my amped-up version of this classic, but I know he would have loved it. It's fun to take this traditional dessert and turn it on its ear. Roasting the bananas gives them an almost caramelized flavor, and the peanut butter cookies give my childhood idol, Elvis Presley, a nod for his love of a peanut butter–banana sandwich. Top it all off with homemade whipped cream and a drizzle of easy ganache, and you've got banana pudding bliss.

SERVES 4 TO 6

Pudding

Nonstick cooking spray

3 to 4 ripe medium bananas

½ teaspoon ground cinnamon

Kosher salt

½ cup granulated sugar

¼ cup plus 2 tablespoons all-purpose flour

2 large eggs

3 large egg yolks

4 cups whole milk

1 teaspoon vanilla extract

30 to 40 peanut butter sandwich cookies

1 cup heavy cream

2 tablespoons confectioners' sugar

Ganache

4 ounces semisweet chocolate chips or chopped semisweet chocolate

½ cup heavy cream

1 **MAKE THE PUDDING:** Preheat the oven to 425°F. Line a baking sheet with parchment paper and spray the parchment with cooking spray.

2 Thinly slice the bananas crosswise, about ⅛ inch thick. Toss the bananas in a bowl with the cinnamon and a pinch of salt. Place in a single layer on the prepared baking sheet. Bake until the bananas start to brown on the edges, about 10 minutes.

3 In a saucepan, whisk together the granulated sugar, flour, and ½ teaspoon salt. Stir in the eggs and egg yolks, then stir in the milk. Cook, uncovered, stirring often, until the mixture thickens, about 10 minutes. Remove from the heat and stir in the vanilla.

4 Spread a thin layer of the pudding over the bottom of a 1½-quart casserole dish. Arrange a layer of sandwich cookies on top of the pudding, and arrange a third of the roasted banana slices over the cookies. Spread a third of the remaining pudding over the bananas and continue layering the cookies, bananas, and pudding, ending with pudding, so you have 3 layers total. Cover and refrigerate for at least 1 hour or up to overnight.

5 In a medium bowl, whip the cream and confectioners' sugar with a hand mixer to stiff peaks. Spread the whipped cream over the banana pudding.

6 **MAKE THE GANACHE:** Place the chocolate in a heatproof bowl. In a small saucepan, heat the cream over medium heat until hot but not simmering, about 5 minutes. Pour the cream over the chocolate and let it sit for a minute, then stir to melt and combine.

7 Drizzle the ganache over the pudding. Spoon the pudding into bowls and serve chilled or at room temperature.

BANANA SPLIT NACHOS

I love a nacho platter. It's the perfect appetizer to share at a restaurant or at home. I took that classic nacho idea and turned it into dessert. You can really mix these chocolate pie chips with any of your favorite dessert toppings, but I love combining the flavors of a banana split onto a big platter for everyone to share. Take as many bites as you want of this decadent pile of goodness!

SERVES 4 TO 6

1 box (2 crusts) refrigerated pie crusts (I like Pillsbury)

1 egg, beaten

1 (1.38-ounce) packet hot chocolate mix

1 cup heavy cream

1 teaspoon vanilla extract

1 cup milk chocolate chips

2 cups strawberries, hulled and quartered

2 bananas, sliced into ¼-inch-thick rounds

1 quart of your favorite ice cream (I like Neapolitan)

1 (6.5-ounce) can whipped cream

¼ cup stemless maraschino cherries, cut in half

¼ cup roasted almonds, roughly chopped

1 Preheat the oven to 375°F.

2 Unroll each round of pie dough onto a separate sheet of parchment paper. Use a fork to prick the dough all over. Brush both rounds with the beaten egg and sprinkle half the packet of the hot cocoa mix over each. Cut each dough round into 14 to 16 thin wedges, like you are cutting up a pizza, being careful not to cut through the parchment, then separate the wedges slightly. Transfer the dough, still on the parchment, onto baking sheets. Bake until crisp and lightly golden brown on the edges and bottoms, 14 to 16 minutes.

3 While the pie chips bake, in a small saucepan, combine the heavy cream and vanilla and heat over medium heat until steaming but not boiling, about 5 minutes. Place the chocolate chips in a medium heatproof bowl and pour the warm cream over them. Let sit for 1 minute, then stir well until melted and smooth.

4 When the pie chips are ready, place half of them on a large dinner plate. Top with half the strawberries, bananas, and chocolate sauce. Add the remaining chips and top with 6 to 8 scoops of ice cream and the remaining strawberries and bananas. Add some puffs of whipped cream and drizzle it all with chocolate sauce. Sprinkle with the cherries and nuts. Serve immediately, with any leftover chocolate sauce on the side.

Banana
Split
Nachos
239

NO-BAKE RICOTTA ESPRESSO CHEESECAKE

I've never met a cheesecake I didn't like, from the dense, New York–style to the easy no-bake boxed variety. I am not a cheesecake snob! The ricotta cheese in this no-bake cheesecake keeps it light, the chocolate crust keeps it decadent, and the espresso powder makes you feel like you're having your coffee right in the cake. *Of course*, I have coffee with my coffee cheesecake! A word about Amarena cherries: This is not your everyday cherry! Look for these wild dark Italian beauties in rich syrup, often sold in a beautiful reusable porcelain jar, at your local grocery store. They are worth searching for, because they have a deep, sweet flavor unlike any cherries you've ever tasted. The cheesecake is great on its own, but the Amarena cherry topping adds a richness that rivals any fancy bakery cheesecake I've tasted.

◆

SERVES 8 TO 10

Crust

1½ cups chocolate graham cracker crumbs (from about 12 full graham cracker sheets)

2 tablespoons sugar

6 tablespoons (¾ stick) unsalted butter, melted

Filling

½ cup heavy cream

1½ teaspoons unflavored powdered gelatin

½ cup sugar

1 tablespoon instant espresso powder

1 (8-ounce) package cream cheese, at room temperature

1 pound good-quality fresh whole-milk ricotta cheese

1 teaspoon vanilla extract

Topping

1 (21-ounce) jar Amarena cherries in syrup

Juice of ½ lemon

1. **MAKE THE CRUST:** Place the graham crackers and sugar in a food processor and pulse to combine. Drizzle in the melted butter and pulse to combine. The mixture should clump together slightly when pressed between your fingers. Press the mixture firmly and evenly over the bottom of an 8-inch springform pan. Freeze to firm the crust, about 15 minutes.

2. **MEANWHILE, MAKE THE FILLING:** Pour the cream into a small bowl and sprinkle the gelatin over. Let sit to bloom the gelatin, about 5 minutes.

3. Transfer the mixture to a small saucepan and add the sugar and espresso powder. Warm over very low heat, whisking continuously just to dissolve the gelatin. Don't let the mixture simmer or boil. Remove from the heat, whisk until completely smooth, and let cool, about 5 minutes.

4. In the bowl of a stand mixer fitted with the paddle attachment, beat the cream cheese on medium-high speed until light and smooth, 2 to 4 minutes. Add the ricotta and beat just until smooth, scraping down the sides of the bowl with a rubber spatula to ensure even mixing.

5. Add the cooled cream-gelatin mixture and the vanilla and beat again until just smooth. Scrape the mixture into the crust and smooth the top. Cover the cheesecake and chill until set, at least 3 hours or overnight.

6. **JUST BEFORE SERVING, MAKE THE TOPPING:** In a small saucepan, warm the cherries and their syrup over low heat. Remove from the heat and stir in the lemon juice.

7. Serve slices of the cheesecake topped with the warm cherry syrup.

TRISHA'S TIP

What does it mean to "bloom" gelatin? As the gelatin absorbs the heavy cream, each granule will enlarge or puff up. This process helps the gelatin dissolve evenly when heated.

DOUBLE-STUFFED BROWNIES

Some recipe ideas come to me in a dream. Really! I love to think of my favorite foods and figure out a way to combine them into something even better. These brownies came from my absolute love of homemade brownies, mixed with my obsession with the double-stuffed Oreo. It's that simple. These creamy stuffed brownies are my tribute to the indescribable goodness of the inside of the famous cookie, sandwiched between my mama's traditional brownies. You are most welcome!

MAKES 12 BROWNIES

Brownies

⅔ cup solid vegetable shortening (I like Crisco sticks), plus more for greasing the pan

4 ounces unsweetened baking chocolate, roughly chopped

4 large eggs

2 cups granulated sugar

2 teaspoons vanilla extract

1⅓ cups all-purpose flour

1 teaspoon baking powder

1 teaspoon kosher salt

Filling

½ cup solid vegetable shortening (I like Crisco sticks)

½ teaspoon vanilla extract

3½ cups confectioners' sugar

3 to 4 tablespoons warm water

1 **MAKE THE BROWNIES:** Preheat the oven to 350°F. Grease a rimmed baking sheet with shortening, then line with parchment paper and grease the parchment.

2 In a microwave-safe bowl, melt the shortening and chocolate together, stirring every 30 seconds, until melted and combined. Set aside to cool slightly.

3 In the bowl of a stand mixer fitted with the paddle attachment, beat the eggs well. Add the granulated sugar and vanilla and beat to combine thoroughly, then beat in the chocolate mixture.

4 On a sheet of waxed paper, sift together the flour, baking powder, and salt. Add the flour mixture to the chocolate mixture by big spoonfuls and mix until fully combined. Spread the batter evenly in the prepared pan.

5 Bake the brownies until a toothpick inserted into the center comes out clean, 12 to 15 minutes. Remove from the oven and let cool in the pan for 10 minutes. Release the edges with a butter knife and turn the brownies out onto a cutting board to cool completely.

6 **MAKE THE FILLING:** In the bowl of a stand mixer fitted with the paddle attachment, combine the shortening and vanilla. Add the confectioners' sugar, 1 cup at a time, adding 1 tablespoon warm water after each addition and mixing until you get a spreadable consistency. You may not need all the water.

7 Cut the brownie slab in half horizontally, creating two large, equal pieces. Spread the filling over one of the large brownie halves and top with the other brownie half like a big sandwich. Cut into 2-inch squares and serve.

DESSERT PIZZA

Beth makes a dessert pizza using cream cheese for the bottom layer. I thought I'd try switching it up and using Nutella, a favorite of our youngest, Allie, and grilling the crust for added flavor. This dessert pizza is one of those very-easy-to-prepare after-supper treats that is so yummy and makes a pretty plate. Top with your favorite fruits and nuts, or try my suggestions here. I use kiwis when they're in season because they were one of my mom's go-to summer fruits. The next time you're summer grilling, throw this crust on the grill for the perfect end to a great day!

SERVES 6 TO 8

16 ounces prepared pizza dough

Canola oil

¾ cup chocolate-hazelnut spread (I like Nutella)

½ cup unsweetened coconut flakes, toasted

¾ cup sliced bananas

¾ cup sliced strawberries

¼ cup sliced kiwi fruit

½ cup chopped roasted salted macadamia nuts

1 Heat a grill to high, trying to get it as hot as possible (500°F).

2 Stretch or roll the pizza dough to fill most of a baking sheet. Brush the grill and the dough with oil. Flip the pizza dough directly onto the grill, oiled-side down. Grill for 2 to 3 minutes on each side, until the crust is cooked through and golden, oiling the other side of the dough before flipping.

3 Remove the crust from the grill and, while it is still hot, spread on the chocolate-hazelnut spread, leaving a ½-inch border. Top with the coconut, bananas, strawberries, kiwi, and nuts. Slice and serve.

PB&J COOKIE BARS

If I'm craving some quick comfort food, I'll make myself a peanut butter and jelly sandwich. I'm a straight-up Jif creamy and Welch's grape jelly gal. Ever since I was a little girl, I have enjoyed these salty-sweet sandwiches, so it was a no-brainer to transform them into dessert bars. Use your favorite peanut butter and your preferred jelly or jam to make these bars your own. The bars store well and are great for a pick-me-up snack or a grab-and-go breakfast.

MAKES 35 BARS

Nonstick cooking spray

4 cups all-purpose flour

2 teaspoons baking powder

1¼ teaspoons kosher salt

1½ cups (3 sticks) unsalted butter, at room temperature

2 cups sugar

3 large eggs

2 teaspoons vanilla extract

1 cup creamy peanut butter

1 cup smooth grape jelly

1 Preheat the oven to 350°F. Line a large (13 x 18-inch) rimmed baking sheet with parchment paper and spray the parchment with cooking spray.

2 On a sheet of waxed paper, whisk together the flour, baking powder, and salt.

3 In the bowl of a stand mixer fitted with the paddle attachment, beat the butter and sugar on medium-high speed until light and fluffy, about 5 minutes.

4 Add the eggs one at a time, beating well after each addition. Beat in the vanilla. Add the flour mixture and beat on low speed until completely incorporated.

5 Dollop the dough in big spoonfuls all over the prepared baking sheet. Loosely cover with plastic wrap and press the dough into an even layer, filling the baking sheet. Remove the plastic wrap.

6 Spoon the peanut butter and jelly all over the cookie dough. Use the back of the spoon to swirl the peanut butter and jelly together, gently pushing them into the surface of the dough.

7 Bake until the cookie is lightly puffed and golden brown at the edges, 20 to 25 minutes. Let cool in the pan before cutting into squares.

Trisha's Tip

To keep the parchment in place while you're dolloping the cookie dough, dab a little bit of the dough under each corner of the parchment and press down to adhere it to the pan.

POTATO CHIP BACON BROWNIES

The name really says all you need to know about these brownies. I haven't met a soul who doesn't love the combination of the saltiness of bacon and potato chips with the sweet decadence of chocolate. These brownies are one of my most requested desserts to take to a party or covered dish supper. Saving some of the bacon crumbles and crushed chips to sprinkle over the top lets everybody know what they're going to find inside when they bite into one. Trust me, these brownies will become a family favorite.

MAKES 16 BROWNIES

Nonstick cooking spray

8 slices bacon, cut into ½-inch pieces

1 cup (2 sticks) unsalted butter

2 cups sugar

¾ cup unsweetened cocoa powder

2 teaspoons vanilla extract

1 teaspoon baking powder

½ teaspoon kosher salt

4 large eggs

1¼ cups all-purpose flour

1½ cups semisweet chocolate chips

2½ cups lightly crushed ridged potato chips

1 Preheat the oven to 350°F. Line a 9 x 13-inch baking pan with parchment paper, leaving a 3-inch overhang on all sides. Spray the parchment with cooking spray.

2 In a medium skillet, cook the bacon over medium heat, stirring often, until very crispy, about 10 minutes. Drain on paper towels. Reserve the fat in the skillet.

3 Add the butter to the skillet with the bacon fat and melt over medium heat. Add the sugar and stir until it starts to dissolve, about 1 minute. Turn off the heat and let the mixture cool for 2 to 3 minutes.

4 In the bowl of an electric mixer fitted with the paddle attachment, beat together the cocoa powder, vanilla, baking powder, salt, and eggs until smooth, about 5 minutes, then beat in the cooled butter mixture.

5 Add the flour and stir until just incorporated. Remove the bowl from the mixer and fold in the chocolate chips, half the bacon, and 1 cup of the potato chips. Scoop into the prepared baking pan and smooth with an offset spatula. Sprinkle with the remaining bacon and chips, pressing them lightly onto the surface of the batter.

6 Bake until a toothpick inserted into the center of the brownies comes out with a few crumbs attached, 25 to 30 minutes. Let cool in the pan for 15 minutes, then transfer to a cutting board and cut into squares.

PEACH SKILLET CROSTATA

My sister, Beth, has a peach orchard on her farm, and she grows a variety of peaches. Now, we Georgia girls love a peach, whether it be the traditional yellow, the beautiful blush-white, freestone or clingstone. Peaches ripen during late June through July and August, so look for them at your local grocery store or farmers market. We serve our skillet crostata all summer long with a scoop of vanilla ice cream or a dollop of rich whipped cream!

SERVES 8

Crust

1½ cups all-purpose flour, plus more for dusting

2 tablespoons light brown sugar

1 teaspoon kosher salt

6 tablespoons (¾ stick) unsalted butter, cubed and chilled

¼ cup ice water

Filling

5 large fresh peaches, peeled, pitted, and sliced (5 cups)

1 tablespoon fresh lemon juice

3 tablespoons cornstarch

½ cup packed light brown sugar

½ teaspoon ground cinnamon

Pinch of kosher salt

2 tablespoons heavy cream

Turbinado sugar, for sprinkling

1 **MAKE THE CRUST:** In a medium bowl, mix the flour, brown sugar, and salt together with a fork. Cut in the cold butter using a pastry blender or two butter knives until the dough is crumbly and resembles coarse meal. Add the ice water 1 tablespoon at a time and mix in with the fork until the dough begins to come together.

2 Turn the dough out onto a flour-dusted work surface and shape it into a disc. Wrap the disc in plastic wrap and refrigerate for at least 1 hour.

3 **MEANWHILE, MAKE THE FILLING:** In a large bowl, combine the peaches, lemon juice, cornstarch, brown sugar, cinnamon, and salt and gently stir together with a spatula until the peaches are fully coated. Set aside.

4 Preheat the oven to 400°F.

5 Take the pie dough out of the refrigerator and let it sit on the counter for 15 minutes to soften a little, then, on a lightly floured surface, roll the dough out into a rough 10-inch round. Carefully transfer the dough to an 8-inch cast-iron skillet, letting the excess dough hang over the edge of the skillet. Layer the peach slices in concentric (side-by-side) circles over the crust. Gently fold the edges of the dough over onto the outer edge of the peaches. Brush the exposed dough with the cream, then sprinkle generously with the turbinado sugar.

6 Bake for 45 to 50 minutes, until the crust is golden brown and the filling is bubbling. Let cool for 15 minutes before serving.

 TRISHA'S TIPS

Turbinado sugar is made from sugarcane. It's brown because it contains some molasses, and it's much coarser than refined white sugar. Think Sugar In The Raw!

You can make this crust in a food processor, but be careful not to overmix.

The dough can be made ahead and stored in the refrigerator for up to 2 weeks or in the freezer for up to 3 months.

TIRAMISU AFFOGATO

This is the story of my niece Ashley's first trip to the liquor store! Do tell! The first time Mama, Beth, and I made tiramisu, we were at Beth's house in Tifton, Georgia. We needed Kahlúa, which is a coffee rum liqueur, for the recipe. Tift County is a dry county, so we loaded up the car and drove to "the line." Right across the county line in Enigma, Georgia, we drove to the Whiskey Barrel and got our Kahlúa! It was quite the adventure, with a very young Ashley sitting in the back seat wondering what all the fuss was about! You can use any rum in this recipe, but the coffee in Kahlúa enhances the flavor, so I highly recommend it. If you don't have a barista living at home (I wish I did!), you can buy espresso at a local coffee shop, or just brew an extra strong pot of coffee. *Affogato* is Italian for "drowned," so drowning this classic dessert in a generous pour of espresso will change the way you eat tiramisu forever!

SERVES 9

2 cups heavy cream

½ cup plus 2 tablespoons sugar

2 teaspoons vanilla extract

1 (8-ounce) package cream cheese, at room temperature (see Tip)

1 tablespoon instant espresso powder

4 teaspoons Kahlúa or rum

4 cups brewed espresso: 1 cup cold, 2 to 3 cups hot

1 (7-ounce) package hard ladyfingers (about 24)

1 quart vanilla ice cream

1 In the bowl of a stand mixer fitted with the whisk attachment, whip the cream, ¼ cup of the sugar, and 1 teaspoon of the vanilla until soft peaks form, about 5 minutes. Do not whip the cream too stiff. It needs to still be soft when you fold it into the cream cheese. Transfer the whipped cream to a medium bowl and refrigerate.

2 Switch to the paddle attachment and, in the same mixer bowl, beat the cream cheese, ¼ cup of the sugar, the remaining 1 teaspoon vanilla, and the espresso powder until smooth and well combined. Fold the whipped cream into the cream cheese mixture and set aside.

3 In a shallow bowl, mix the remaining 2 tablespoons sugar, the Kahlúa, and the 1 cup cold espresso for 1 to 2 minutes, until the sugar has dissolved. Dip each ladyfinger into the espresso mixture to coat on all sides. Line the entire bottom of an 8-inch square cake pan with an even layer of the dipped ladyfingers. Top with half the cream mixture, spreading it evenly across the top. Repeat with another layer of dipped ladyfingers and then the remaining cream mixture. Cover with plastic wrap and chill for 2 to 3 hours or up to overnight.

4 Spoon a generous serving of the chilled tiramisu into the bottom of a shallow bowl, top with a scoop of vanilla ice cream, then pour over some hot espresso and serve immediately. Repeat for the remaining servings.

TRISHA'S TIPS

I substitute cream cheese for the classic mascarpone used in most tiramisu because I usually have some on hand in the fridge. Feel free to use what you like!

Store-bought ladyfingers range from soft and spongy to hard and crunchy. The harder variety are less likely to fall apart when dipped in espresso.

FRUITCAKE BARS

If "fruitcake" sends you running for cover, you're not alone! Some of us think of that log of fruitcake from the '70s that our parents seemed to get as a gift every holiday, which just sat on the kitchen counter, untouched. My dad said it would make a great door stop! I promise you, you're going to rethink your position on fruitcake when you taste these fruity, nutty bars of goodness. Beth made these for herself, thinking they'd be a healthy grab-and-go snack, and then noticed that they were quickly disappearing—as her guys discovered them on the kitchen counter. They're quick to make with ingredients you probably already have in the pantry.

MAKES 16 BARS

⅓ cup all-purpose flour

½ teaspoon kosher salt

½ teaspoon baking powder

⅓ cup raw cane sugar

2 cups pecans, roughly chopped

1 cup dates, pitted and roughly chopped into big pieces

1 cup dried apricots, roughly chopped into big pieces

½ cup dried figs, hard tips removed and roughly chopped into big pieces

1 large egg

1 tablespoon molasses

¼ teaspoon almond extract

¼ teaspoon vanilla extract

1   Preheat the oven to 325°F. Line an 8-inch square pan with aluminum foil, leaving enough hanging over the edges so you can lift out the bars later, and coat the foil with nonstick spray.

2   In a large bowl, whisk together the flour, salt, baking powder, and raw sugar. Toss in the pecans, dates, apricots, and figs.

3   In a small bowl, whisk together the egg, molasses, and almond and vanilla extracts. Pour the egg mixture over the dry mixture and stir together until fully blended. The mixture will seem dry at first, but keep mixing until the flour incorporates. The batter will be thick and chunky. Press the batter into the prepared pan, pushing it to fill in the corners and flattening it with the back of a spoon.

4   Bake for 35 to 40 minutes, until the bars are dark golden brown and look as though they have pulled away from the sides of the pan. Let cool in the pan for 15 minutes, then lift out onto a cutting board and let cool completely. Cut into bars and store in an airtight container for up to two weeks.

Dried fruit comes in a range of dryness. This recipe benefits from a good soft chew, so when selecting your dates, figs, and apricots, give them a squeeze to make sure they aren't too dry.

If you prefer to use different fruits or nuts, go for it! Just make sure you use the same amounts so you get a good balance of fruit and nut in your bars.

PEAR CRANBERRY WALNUT QUICK BREAD

When bags of fresh cranberries start showing up in the produce department, I start thinking about my favorite fall quick breads. This recipe combines some of the best—cranberries, pears, and walnuts—into a bread that Garth has been quick to finish off (quick bread—get it??). And that touch of apple pie spice in the batter makes my kitchen smell like autumn's on the way. This is a delicious alternative to banana bread.

SERVES 10

1 cup walnut halves

Nonstick cooking spray

¾ cup all-purpose flour

¾ cup whole wheat flour

1 teaspoon baking soda

½ teaspoon kosher salt

¾ cup sugar

¾ teaspoon apple pie spice (see Tips)

3 medium Bosc pears

1 large egg

½ cup canola oil

Zest of 1 lemon

1 tablespoon fresh lemon juice

1 teaspoon vanilla extract

1 cup fresh or frozen cranberries (see Tips), thawed, well drained, and patted dry if frozen

1 Preheat the oven to 350°F, with a rack in the middle.

2 Place the walnuts in an even layer on a small baking sheet and bake for 6 to 8 minutes, until fragrant and toasted, giving them a shake halfway through. Keep a close eye on the walnuts, because they can easily burn. Let cool slightly. When cool enough to handle, roughly chop and set aside.

3 Reduce the oven temperature to 325°F. Spray a 9 x 5-inch glass loaf pan with cooking spray.

4 In a medium bowl, whisk together the all-purpose flour, whole wheat flour, baking soda, salt, sugar, and apple pie spice.

5 Peel the pears and grate into a rimmed baking sheet or shallow bowl to reserve the juices so you get 1½ cups of pulp and juice. Put the grated pears and their juices to a large bowl. Add the egg, oil, lemon zest, lemon juice, and vanilla and whisk to combine, then add the dry mixture in two parts until fully combined. Fold in the walnuts and cranberries until they are evenly dispersed. Pour the mixture into the prepared loaf pan and bake in the middle of the oven rack for 1 hour 10 minutes, or until the bread has domed and a toothpick inserted into the center comes out clean. Since there is fresh fruit in the loaf, test it with the toothpick in two or three places. You might put the toothpick into a cranberry and think it's not baked.

6 Let cool in the pan for 30 minutes, then gently transfer from the pan to a wire rack and let cool completely.

If you don't have apple pie spice, make your own! For 1 teaspoon apple pie spice, combine ½ teaspoon ground cinnamon, ¼ teaspoon freshly grated or ground nutmeg, ⅛ teaspoon ground allspice, and a dash of ground cloves.

If you can't find fresh or frozen cranberries at your grocery store, substitute ¾ cup dried cranberries. To rehydrate them, cover with water in a small saucepan, bring to a boil, then remove from the heat and let sit for 20 minutes. Drain and add to the recipe.

CREAM CHEESE POUND CAKE

Every time I think I've settled on the perfect pound cake, along comes one to challenge it. Beth and I had a "who made this?" moment when we tasted this cake at a family reunion, and we didn't rest until we tracked down the baker. Our cousin Tracy Paulk Griffin was happy to share her great-grandmother, Vera Lott's, recipe—many thanks! Cream cheese gives this pound cake some serious flavor, moistness, and texture. And hey—there's no rule that says we can only have one perfect pound cake recipe!

MAKES 12 SERVINGS

1½ cups (3 sticks) unsalted butter, at room temperature, plus more for greasing

1 (8-ounce) package cream cheese, at room temperature

3 cups sugar

Pinch of fine sea salt

1½ teaspoons vanilla extract

6 large eggs, at room temperature

3 cups sifted cake flour

1 Grease a nonstick 10-inch tube pan with butter.

2 In the bowl of a stand mixer fitted with the paddle attachment, cream the butter, cream cheese, and sugar on high speed until light and fluffy, about 2 minutes, scraping the bowl to help incorporate as needed.

3 Add the salt and vanilla, mixing for a few seconds to combine. With the mixer on low speed, add the eggs one at a time, beating well after each addition and scraping the bowl as needed. With the mixer on low speed, add the flour in two additions, stirring until combined, scraping one last time if needed. Pour the batter into the prepared pan, tapping the pan on the counter once or twice to settle the batter.

4 Place the pan on the center rack in a cold oven. Turn the oven on to 325°F and bake for 1 hour 20 minutes, or until golden brown on top and a toothpick inserted into the cake comes out clean. Let cool in the pan for 10 minutes and then transfer to a wire rack to cool completely.

TRISHA'S TIPS

Why start with a cold oven? The reason you preheat an oven is to allow lighter cakes to rise quickly, but then quickly kill the leavening ingredients so the cake doesn't spill out over the inside of your oven. Pound cakes are so dense that they don't rise much, so that initial blast of heat isn't needed. A cold oven allows the cake batter to rise with the oven temperature, which gives you a fully cooked pound cake with a gorgeous thick crust.

This recipe was written long before convection ovens were a thing. If you have an oven with a convection option, even if you choose the regular bake option, the convection fans will come on, making it hard for the proper rise to happen in a cold oven. If that's you, preheat your oven to 325°F and bake for one hour or until a toothpick inserted into the cake comes out clean.

PEANUT BUTTER PIE

One year, instead of asking for his traditional German chocolate birthday cake, Beth's husband, John, went rogue and asked for a peanut butter pie instead, remembering one they had enjoyed at a wedding reception. They sat down and wrote out all their memories of that decadent pie, which included chocolate sauce, peanut butter, and chocolate–peanut butter candy—resulting in our version of a classic. This peanut butter pie totally filled the bill for John's birthday wish. We love the crunch the Reese's Pieces give this creamy pie. I love creating new recipes from tastes I've enjoyed along the way, and then having them become new family traditions. Thanks, John!

SERVES 8

Crust

Nonstick cooing spray

1½ cups finely ground graham cracker crumbs

3 tablespoons sugar

Pinch of kosher salt

6 tablespoons (¾ stick) unsalted butter, melted

Filling

8 ounces mascarpone cheese

2¼ cups heavy whipping cream

1½ cups confectioners' sugar, sifted

1¾ cups smooth peanut butter (avoid natural peanut butter), plus 2 tablespoons for topping

½ cup Reese's Pieces candies

1 **MAKE THE CRUST:** Preheat the oven to 375°F. Lightly spray a 9-inch glass pie plate with cooking spray.

2 In a medium bowl, whisk together the graham cracker crumbs, sugar, and salt. Stir in the melted butter to fully combine until the mixture resembles wet sand. Pour the mixture into the prepared pie plate and press to compact it into an even layer; be sure to really pack it down. A great way to press the crust in the pie plate is by using a ½-cup measure to push it against the bottom and edges of the plate. Bake the crust for 15 to 18 minutes, until lightly golden, then let cool. Refrigerate until completely chilled before filling.

3 **MAKE THE FILLING:** In the bowl of a stand mixer fitted with the paddle attachment, combine half the mascarpone, the cream, and ¾ cup of the confectioners' sugar and whip until it forms stiff peaks, 5 to 7 minutes. Transfer the whipped cream to a large bowl and set aside.

4 In the mixer bowl, combine the remaining mascarpone, the peanut butter, and the remaining ¾ cup confectioners' sugar and blend together, 1½ to 2 minutes. Add half the whipped cream and whip on medium-high speed to combine, another 2 minutes, pausing halfway to scrape down the sides as the peanut butter mix is sticky and can get stuck. The mixture should be like a light, fluffy mousse. Spoon the filling into the chilled crust and gently spread it to the edges using the back of the spoon.

5 Transfer the remaining whipped cream to a piping bag fitted with a medium star tip. Pipe the whipped cream over the filling, winding back and forth from the outer edge of the pie 2 inches toward the center, making sure to leave an inner circle to fill in with Reese's Pieces later. Chill the pie uncovered in the refrigerator for at least 5 hours or up to overnight.

6 When you're ready to serve, warm 2 tablespoons peanut butter and drizzle over the top of the pie, then fill the center with the Reese's Pieces.

GRANNY'S TEA CAKES

Beth and I are always in search of the perfect tea cake. For us, that means big round cakes that are soft in the middle, not firm and snappy! Our family friend Mrs. Helen Carter, of skillet apple pie fame, offered us her recipe for her tea cakes, and we knew they would fit the bill! Our grandmother Lizzie used to make everything from biscuits to tea cakes in a large, shallow-bottomed wooden bread bowl, which Mrs. Carter also recommends. Most of us don't have those, so I use my clean countertop to put this sweet, simple dough together, but I left the instructions in the recipe, because it reminded me of my grandma. Beth and I added the sugar drizzle because we wanted to go the extra mile, but these tender tea cakes are just fine on their own!

◆

MAKES 20 COOKIES

2 cups sifted self-rising flour, plus more for dusting

¼ teaspoon baking powder

1 cup granulated sugar

½ cup whole milk

1 teaspoon vanilla extract

1 egg

½ cup solid vegetable shortening (I like Crisco)

½ cup confectioners' sugar

2 to 3 tablespoons buttermilk

1 Preheat the oven to 350°F. Line two baking sheets with parchment paper.

2 Sift the flour and baking powder into a medium bowl, then add the granulated sugar and stir to mix.

3 Make a well in the center of the dry mixture, and add the milk, vanilla, egg, and shortening. Stir well to combine into a very stiff, but sticky batter.

4 Spread some flour in a flat-bottomed bowl or on your countertop. Then dip heaping tablespoons of dough and drop them into the flour one at a time. Using your hands, roll the dough to just coat it with flour and shape it into a ball, approximately ¾ inch round. Place it on one prepared baking sheet and flatten it out with your hands to about a ½-inch thickness, trying not to overhandle the dough. Repeat with the rest of the cookie dough, making approximately 1½-inch rounds, spaced about 1½ inches apart on the two baking sheets.

5 Bake for 10 to 12 minutes, until they are just starting to brown at the edges but are still very light, but dry, on top. Switch the pans (top and bottom) and rotate them 180 degrees halfway through baking.

6 Remove from the oven and let cool on the pans for 2 to 3 minutes, then carefully transfer the cookies to a wire rack to cool completely.

7 Once the cookies have cooled, make the glaze: In a small bowl, stir together the confectioners' sugar and 1 tablespoon of the buttermilk to combine. Slowly add more buttermilk a little at a time until the glaze is pourable but will hold a thick line when drizzled, not spread out flat.

8 Drizzle the glaze over the tea cakes and let set for 20 minutes before serving. If you're not eating these cookies right away, make sure to pack them up in an airtight container so they stay tender. Store for up to two weeks.

ASHLEY'S CUPCAKES

When Ashley was a week old, Mama made these cupcakes to celebrate her one-week birthday (Kyle and Bret still roll their eyes at that one!). In the photos of that day, we thought week-old Ashley resembled a little tree frog, so these became the "tree frog cupcakes." Ashley has requested this cake in various forms for her birthday over the years. On her eighth birthday, my mom and dad took the family to a Macon Braves baseball game, and Mama brought these cupcakes for the occasion. Grammy thought she'd match the dessert with the gift bag she was bringing, and brought Ashley's present in a colorful cupcake bag. On closer inspection at the party, everyone noticed that the images on the bag weren't cupcakes . . . can I say "boobs" in a cookbook? And the story of Ashley's inappropriate birthday lives in infamy!

MAKES 12 CUPCAKES

Cupcakes

⅔ cup granulated sugar

¼ teaspoon kosher salt

½ cup (1 stick) butter, melted and cooled slightly

2 large eggs, at room temperature

⅔ cup milk

1 teaspoon vanilla extract

1¾ cups all-purpose flour

1½ teaspoons baking powder

Chocolate Buttercream

2 cups confectioners' sugar

½ cup unsweetened cocoa powder

4 tablespoons (½ stick) butter, at room temperature

¼ cup milk, plus more to thin the frosting if needed

1 teaspoon vanilla extract

1 **MAKE THE CUPCAKES:** Preheat the oven to 350°F, with a rack in the middle. Line a 12-cup muffin tin with cupcake liners.

2 In a large bowl, combine the granulated sugar and salt, then whisk in the melted butter just to combine. Add the eggs one at a time and whisk until the mixture is light and fluffy, about 2 minutes. Whisk in the milk and vanilla. Sift in the flour and baking powder and stir to combine.

3 Fill each cupcake liner evenly, about 3 tablespoons each. Bake for 18 to 22 minutes, until the cupcakes are lightly golden brown and the tops pop back when lightly pressed.

4 Let the cupcakes cool in the pan for 5 minutes, then transfer to a wire rack to cool completely before frosting.

5 **MEANWHILE, MAKE THE BUTTERCREAM:** In a medium bowl, whisk together the confectioners' sugar and cocoa powder. Add the butter, milk, and vanilla. Beat on low speed using a hand mixer until the mixture comes together, then increase the speed to combine into a smooth, spreadable frosting. Thin with more milk if needed.

6 Dollop or pipe the buttercream onto the cupcakes and serve. Store in an airtight container at room temperature for up to 1 week.

This old-school recipe doesn't call for a stand mixer, but you can make the cupcake batter and the frosting using one if you prefer.

PRINCESS CAKE

I LOVE chef Mary Berry! She was a joy to behold on the first few seasons of *The Great British Bake Off*, where she was judge and jury! I became an instant fan of Mary, from her English accent (I do a terrible impersonation!) to her friendly yet firm manner when critiquing food. I was so inspired by Mary's gorgeous Swedish layer cake, called a *prinsesstårta* (princess cake) that I decided to try to make my own version. I roped Beth and her daughter Ashley into helping me. We were so proud to have actually made the cake that we could've stopped there, but it looked so yummy, someone had to taste it. I cut the cake for Garth and his best friend Randy to try and they were absolutely blown away. The sponge cake is light and moist, and the combination of custard and cream, mixed with the jam, is really something special. This cake is definitely a showstopper! I make this Mary Berry–inspired homemade marzipan because I like the sweet almond flavoring, but you can make it super easy on yourself and order plain white fondant online, color it, and call it a day.

◆

SERVES 8 TO 10

Custard

1¼ cups milk

3 extra-large egg yolks

¼ cup granulated sugar

¼ cup cornstarch

2 teaspoons vanilla extract

2 tablespoons unsalted butter

Cake

Nonstick cooking spray

3 tablespoons unsalted butter

4 extra-large eggs

¾ cup granulated sugar

⅔ cup cornstarch

½ cup plus 2 tablespoons all-purpose flour

1 teaspoon baking powder

Filling and Topping

6 ounces of your favorite jam (try Beth's Peach Preserves, page 213)

4 cups heavy whipping cream

Marzipan

2 cups finely ground almond flour

1½ cups confectioners' sugar, sifted, plus more for dusting

1 extra-large egg white

1 teaspoon clear vanilla extract

Lime-green and pink gel food coloring (or colors of your choosing)

1 **MAKE THE CUSTARD:** In a medium saucepan, heat the milk over low heat until just simmering, 8 to 10 minutes. Remove from the heat and let cool for 10 minutes.

2 In a medium bowl, whisk together the egg yolks, granulated sugar, and cornstarch. This mixture will be very thick and clumpy at first, but keep whisking until fully incorporated, pale, and creamy. Whisk the warm milk into the egg mixture a little at a time to temper the eggs and keep them from scrambling. Pour the mixture back into the saucepan and cook over medium-low heat, whisking continuously, for 4 to 5 minutes, until the mixture gets very thick. Remove from the heat and add the vanilla and the butter, whisking until the butter is melted and fully incorporated.

3 Transfer the custard to a bowl and cover with plastic wrap, making sure to press down onto the custard's surface to prevent a skin from forming. Let the custard cool for 5 to 10 minutes, then refrigerate until completely cool while you make the cake.

4 **MAKE THE CAKE:** Preheat the oven to 350°F. Line a rimmed baking sheet with aluminum foil. Spray a 9-inch springform pan with cooking spray, line with parchment, and spray again, then place on the prepared baking sheet.

5 Melt the butter in a microwave-safe bowl and set aside to cool.

Recipe Continues

6 In the bowl of a stand mixer fitted with the whisk attachment, whisk the eggs and granulated sugar for 8 to 10 minutes, until pale, thick, and foamy, and the whisk leaves a trail like a ribbon on the surface when lifted.

7 On a sheet of waxed paper, sift together the cornstarch, flour, and baking powder. Remove the bowl from the mixer and fold in the flour mixture with a large spatula. Fold in the melted butter until just combined. Do not overmix.

8 Pour the batter into the prepared pan and bake for 25 to 30 minutes, until the cake is golden brown and starts to come away from the sides of the pan. Remove from the oven and let cool in the pan for 10 minutes. Loosen the cake from the pan by running a butter knife around the edges of the cake, then release the springform ring and transfer the cake to a wire rack to cool completely.

9 **TO ASSEMBLE THE CAKE:** cut it horizontally into three even layers. Place one of the layers on a cake platter and spread a thin layer of custard over the top. Spoon about ½ cup of the remaining custard into a piping bag, snip off the tip of the bag at about ½ inch, and pipe a border around the edge of the cake. (This creates a "wall" to keep the preserves from oozing out of the cake.) Spread the jam inside the custard border.

10 **MAKE THE FILLING:** In the bowl of a stand mixer fitted with the paddle attachment, whip 3½ cups of the cream until firm, 6 to 8 minutes. Fold 1 cup of the whipped cream into the remaining custard and spread one-third of the custard cream over the jam layer, then top with the second cake layer. Cover with the remaining custard cream and top with the final cake layer. Cover the sides of the cake with a thin layer of whipped cream, smoothing it like frosting, then dollop the remaining whipped cream on the top of the cake and smooth it into a dome shape. Freeze the cake for 30 minutes to set the whipped cream.

Recipe Continues

11 **MEANWHILE, MAKE THE MARZIPAN:** In the bowl of a stand mixer fitted with the dough hook, mix the almond flour and confectioners' sugar until combined. Add the egg white and the vanilla and mix until a dough is formed, about 2 minutes. Pinch out 4 tablespoons of the dough and set aside. Add 4 to 6 drops of lime-green food color to the dough and mix until it starts to incorporate. (The mixer will help get the color started in the marzipan but you will finish kneading the color through once you take the marzipan out of the mixer).

12 Turn the marzipan out onto a clean work surface generously sprinkled with confectioners' sugar. Knead until the color is uniform and the marzipan comes together. Add more lime-green food coloring to get your desired color.

13 Roll the marzipan out into a round roughly 16 inches in diameter, large enough to cover the cake, and about ⅛ inch thick.

14 Remove the cake from the freezer, carefully lift the green marzipan up and over the cake, and, using your hands, gently shape the marzipan around the cake until it's smooth. Trim off any excess.

15 Making sure to clean up any green bits on your work surface, then sprinkle with a little more confectioners' sugar and knead the reserved 4 tablespoons marzipan, adding 1 or 2 drops of pink food coloring until you get a light pink marzipan.

16 Roll the pink marzipan into a "snake" that is about 6 inches long and ½ inch round. Cut the rope crosswise into ½-inch pieces. Roll each piece into a ball, then place them about 2 inches apart on a piece of plastic wrap. Cover with another piece of plastic wrap and push down on each ball with your thumb to flatten them into thin circles. Working through the plastic wrap, press one edge of the flattened ball to form the thin edge of a petal, leaving the other edge thicker. Repeat for each ball. Remove the top piece of plastic and, using your fingers, roll a petal up to form the bud. Add each petal, pushing the thicker end to the bottom and the thin edge upward until you form a rose. With your fingers, gently push out each petal so the rose shape looks more like a blooming flower. Cut the excess marzipan from the bottom of the rose. Set aside.

17 Whip the remaining ½ cup cream, spoon into a piping bag fitted with a star tip, and pipe around the base of the cake.

18 Dust the dome of the cake with confectioners' sugar and top with the pink rose. Store leftover cake covered in the refrigerator for up to 1 week.

TRISHA'S TIP

Place your stand mixer bowl and whisk attachment in the freezer for 30 minutes before whisking heavy cream. A cold bowl, cold whisk, and cold cream make whipped cream in half the time!

Trisha's Notes on Marzipan

1 Buy finely ground almond flour in the baking section of your grocery store, or make your own by putting 2 cups slivered almonds in a food processor or high-speed blender and pulsing until you achieve a fine flour. Use blanched slivered almonds instead of whole almonds with their skins to keep the marzipan light in color for tinting.

2 Use disposable kitchen gloves when working with food coloring so you don't dye your hands!

3 Using egg whites and clear vanilla extract keeps the marzipan white so you can more accurately get the color you want when you tint it.

4 You don't have to refrigerate the marzipan before adding it to this cake, but it will firm a little when colder, so making it a day ahead is a good idea. Just be sure to let it sit on the counter to come up to room temperature before rolling.

5 Wrap any leftover marzipan in plastic wrap, then place in a resealable bag, pressing out all the air as you seal the bag. Store in the refrigerator for up to 3 weeks.

6 Mary Berry says to make sure to use gel, not liquid, food coloring, so that's what I do!

UNCLE WILSON'S ICE CREAM "THING"

My uncle Wilson was famous for bringing this cold dessert to every family get-together. When he gave me the "recipe" there were no amounts listed—he said it was more of an eyeball thing, so . . . use your imagination to create your own ice cream "thing"! We ate this decadent dessert right out of the pan, but I turn it out onto a platter and top with additional whipped cream, cherries, nuts, and blueberries for a pretty presentation. Uncle Wilson sometimes used Cool Whip in the bottom layer instead of whipped cream. My friend Mandy substitutes Neapolitan ice cream as the bottom layer. Try it!

SERVES 10

2 cups heavy whipping cream

1 teaspoon vanilla extract

3 tablespoons confectioners' sugar

10 ice cream sandwiches

½ cup chocolate fudge syrup

½ cup caramel or butterscotch syrup

1 cup mixed nuts, finely chopped, plus 2 tablespoons chopped for topping

1 cup whole maraschino cherries

1 (6.5-ounce) can whipped cream

½ cup blueberries

Special Equipment
9-cup large rectangular food storage container (I used a 9-cup Ziploc tub)

1 Chill the bowl of a stand mixer in the freezer. Line a large (9-cup) rectangular food storage container with a piece of trimmed parchment paper leaving about 4 inches overhanging both long sides of the tub so you can lift the dessert after it's frozen.

2 In the chilled bowl of the stand mixer fitted with the paddle attachment, whip the cream, vanilla, and confectioners' sugar to stiff peaks, about 5 minutes.

3 In the prepared container, layer one-quarter of the whipped cream, then 5 of the ice cream sandwiches, then another quarter of the whipped cream. Drizzle a layer of fudge sauce and another drizzle of caramel or butterscotch syrup, ½ cup of the nuts, then evenly distribute all but 10 of the cherries over the top. Add half the remaining whipped cream and the remaining 5 ice cream sandwiches. Repeat the layering with the remaining whipped cream, fudge sauce, and caramel or butterscotch syrup, and remaining ½ cup nuts.

4 Freeze until ready to serve, at least 4 hours, then let sit out for 5 minutes before serving. Release from the container by running a flat butter knife around the edges and lifting it out. Peel off the parchment and set on a platter. Spray two rows of 5 puffs of canned whipped cream along the top and dot those with the reserved 10 cherries. Sprinkle with the last 2 tablespoons nuts and the blueberries.

5 To serve, run a sharp knife under hot water, dry it, then slice.

JANINE'S NO-BAKES

Ashley met her friend Janine when they attended graduate nursing school together at Vanderbilt here in Nashville. Yes, I'm a proud aunt! Janine made these no-bakes one afternoon and brought them over to hang out and watch Garth's (and Janine's!) favorite team, the Pittsburgh Steelers, play football. Garth ate every single one. Every. Single. One. I'm not even kidding. I make these no-bakes for Garth now every time we watch the Steelers play. It's become tradition, thanks to Janine.

MAKES 26

2 cups sugar

3 tablespoons unsweetened cocoa powder

½ cup (1 stick) butter, cut into 5 or 6 pieces

½ cup milk

¾ cup smooth peanut butter

1 teaspoon vanilla extract

3 cups rolled oats (I prefer Quaker old-fashioned oats)

1 Line two baking sheets with waxed paper, and measure all your ingredients, because these no-bakes come together quickly and you will want to be ready.

2 In a medium saucepot, stir together the sugar, cocoa powder, butter, and milk. Heat over high heat, stirring continuously, until the mixture comes to a boil, 4 to 5 minutes. As soon as the mixture comes to a boil, start a timer for 2 minutes and continue stirring. The mixture will bubble vigorously.

3 As soon as the timer is up, remove the pan from the heat and add the peanut butter. Stir until melted, about 2 minutes. As the peanut butter melts, stir in the vanilla, then stir in the oats to fully combine.

4 Drop the mixture in heaping tablespoonfuls onto the prepared baking sheets and let set for 20 to 25 minutes. Store in an airtight container at room temperature.

Granny's
Tea Cakes
260

Fruitcake
Bars
253

Janine's
No-Bakes

COCONUT CREAM PIE

Garth and I have a longtime friend named Carol who lives in Arlington and works at Six Flags Over Texas. One year for my birthday, we were on tour in Dallas and she helped Garth surprise me by opening up the park after hours. I LOVE roller coasters, and Six Flags Over Texas has several. Garth, myself, Carol, the band, and the crew got to ride roller coasters for hours, with no lines! It was the most fun birthday I've had, in a string of fun birthdays! Carol is quiet and shy and never asks for anything, but I wanted to say thank you. I found out her favorite dessert is coconut cream pie, and I make this decadent, whipped cream–topped concoction for every birthday I get to spend with her.

SERVES 8

1 (9-inch) unbaked deep-dish pie crust, homemade (recipe follows) or store-bought

6 large egg yolks

⅓ cup cornstarch

¾ cup granulated sugar

1½ cups half-and-half

1 (13.5-ounce) can full-fat coconut milk, well shaken

½ teaspoon kosher salt

1½ cups sweetened shredded coconut

4 tablespoons (½ stick) unsalted butter

1 teaspoon vanilla extract

Nonstick cooking spray

2 cups cold heavy whipping cream

¼ cup confectioners' sugar

1 cup unsweetened coconut flakes, toasted

1 Fully blind bake the pie crust (see the last step of the Homemade Pie Crust recipe on page 274 for instructions on blind baking). Set aside to cool completely.

2 In a medium bowl, whisk together the egg yolks, cornstarch and ¼ cup of the granulated sugar until well combined. Set aside.

3 In a medium saucepan, stir together the half-and-half, coconut milk, remaining ½ cup granulated sugar, and salt. While stirring regularly, bring just to a boil over medium heat, then reduce the heat to low.

4 Remove ½ cup of the coconut milk blend and slowly stream into the egg yolk mixture while whisking continuously to temper the eggs. Slowly stream the tempered egg mixture into the saucepan, and whisk together to combine over low heat. The mixture will thicken almost immediately into a pudding. Remove from the heat. Stir in the sweetened coconut, butter, and vanilla.

5 Pour the filling into the cooled pie crust. Lightly spray a sheet of plastic wrap with cooking spray and press the sprayed side onto the surface of the custard to prevent a skin from forming. Refrigerate for 3 hours or overnight.

6 Using a stand mixer with the whisk attachment, or a hand-held mixer, combine the cream and confectioners' sugar in a medium bowl and whip until stiff peaks form, about 4 minutes.

7 Add the whipped cream to a piping bag with a large round tip and pipe about 1-inch-tall, rounded puffs of whipped cream on top of the set pie filling. Sprinkle with toasted unsweetened coconut flakes.

Recipe Continues

Homemade Pie Crust

¼ cup ice water

1¼ cups sifted all-purpose flour, plus more for dusting

1½ teaspoons granulated sugar

½ teaspoon kosher salt

3 tablespoons unsalted butter, cubed and chilled

6 tablespoons solid vegetable shortening (I like Crisco), cubed and chilled

Pour the water over ice cubes to keep very cold. In a large bowl, add the flour, sugar, and salt and whisk to combine. Add the butter and shortening to the bowl and use a pastry blender or two knives to "cut" or work the fats into the flour mixture until pea-size lumps form. Sprinkle in the ice water, 1 tablespoon at a time, using a fork or your hands to pull the dough together, until the dough becomes just sticky enough to form a ball. You may not need to use all the ice water. Use just enough to make the dough stick together.

Transfer the dough to a clean work surface lightly dusted with flour. Press all the moistened portions together gently and quickly with your fingers. Do not knead. The less the dough is handled, the more tender and flakier the pastry will be. Form the dough into a disc, then wrap with plastic wrap and refrigerate for at least 1 hour. (This step can be done several days in advance.)

When ready to bake, take the dough out of the refrigerator and let it rest for 15 minutes, so it will be easier to roll out. Sprinkle your work surface (I use my clean kitchen counter) and a rolling pin with flour. Preheat the oven to 350°F.

Roll out the dough into a circle that is about ⅛ inch thick and 12 inches in diameter. Gently lay the pie circle over a 9-inch pie plate and center, pushing the dough into the bottom and gently up the sides of the pan. Tuck the excess dough into the pan with your fingers, then make a fluted edge or use a fork to press down the edges all the way around the pan.

Prebake the crust by first pricking holes over the pastry bottom with a fork to prevent air bubbles from forming during baking. Line the crust with a circle of parchment, foil, or even a round coffee filter. Fill with pie weights or dried beans to weigh down the liner. Bake for 15 to 20 minutes, until light golden brown. Let cool completely if using for a no-bake pie.

Makes 1 bottom crust

For a smoother pie filling, pulse the sweetened shredded coconut in a mini food processor before adding it to the filling.

Prebaking or blind baking means baking the crust before filling it. If you skip this step, you will sometimes get a soggy bottom crust. If you're going to bake a pie, I suggest partially baking the crust instead of fully baking. Follow the same instructions, but only bake until the crust is just beginning to brown, 7 to 8 minutes, and then add the pie filling and finish in the oven. If the edges of the crust start to brown too much before the pie has finished baking, cover just the edges loosely with aluminum foil to prevent burning.

Tempering the eggs in this recipe is the simple process of slowly adding some of the warm half-and-half mixture to the eggs to warm them up before adding them to the pan with the rest of the warm mixture, so they mix smoothly. If you add cold eggs to hot liquid, you'll get scrambled eggs!

JACK'S FRIED PIES

My dad, Jack, used to reminisce about small fried apple fritters that his mother, Elizabeth, would make for him when he was a kid. Of course, like many passed-down family recipes, this one wasn't written down anywhere, so Mama went to work, trying to figure out how to make them just like *his* mama had. That's never an easy job, because our childhood memories often make those original flavors impossible to replicate. Beth and I remember those premade dough pockets sitting on the kitchen counter, and Mama frying them up in a cast-iron skillet. We also remember how happy Daddy was with the result. We're not surprised she got it right! Grandma Yearwood always fried with lard, but if that scares you, vegetable oil is perfectly fine!

MAKES 10 PIES

1 tablespoon unsalted butter

2 Granny Smith apples, peeled, cored, and diced in ½-inch pieces

¼ teaspoon ground cinnamon

Pinch of freshly grated nutmeg

Pinch of ground ginger

½ cup packed light brown sugar

½ teaspoon kosher salt

1 tablespoon cornstarch

2 pounds lard or 1½ quarts vegetable oil, for frying

1 box (2 crusts) refrigerated pie crusts (I like Pillsbury)

Special Equipment
4½-inch round cookie cutter

1 In a small sauté pan, melt the butter over medium heat. Add the apples, cinnamon, nutmeg, ginger, brown sugar, salt, and ¼ cup water, stir, and cover to bring to a simmer, 5 to 7 minutes, then cook, uncovered, until the apples are slightly softened, about 4 minutes.

2 In a small bowl, stir together the cornstarch and 1 tablespoon water until combined and pourable. Stream the cornstarch slurry into the apple filling and cook on a low simmer for 2 minutes more, or until the liquid has thickened.

3 Pour the apple mixture into a shallow bowl (a pie plate works great) and cool in the fridge, stirring occasionally, for 25 minutes.

4 Put the lard or vegetable oil in a deep Dutch oven. Clip a deep-fry thermometer to its side and heat the lard over high heat to 360°F.

5 Lay out both rounds of pie dough and use a 4½-inch round cookie cutter to cut four circles from each of them. Gather the scraps, roll out again, and cut out 2 more circles.

6 Fill each round of dough with a heaping tablespoon of the apple filling, then, using a little water on your fingers, wet the edge of the dough and press together into a half-moon. Crimp the edges with the tines of a fork to seal.

7 When all the pies are assembled and the oil is to temperature, fry 3 or 4 pies at a time for 4 to 5 minutes. Transfer the pies to a paper towel–lined tray to drain and cool slightly, then repeat to fry the remaining pies, letting the oil come back up to 360°F between batches. Enjoy warm.

The apple filling can be made the day before and stored in the refrigerator until ready to use.

Acknowledgments

There are a lot of cooks in *Trisha's Kitchen*!

To the folks at Houghton Mifflin Harcourt, thank you for the opportunity, especially editorial director Karen Murgolo, for taking on a new job and a new author in the same week! Special thanks to Tai Blanche for superb art direction and to Laura Palese for designing a book I can be proud of. To editorial assistant Jacqueline Quirk, thank you for taking all of my detailed Virgo notes and bringing them to life in these pages. On the HMH team, thank you to Marina Padakis Lowry, Shara Alexander, Andrea DeWerd, Kimberly Kiefer, and everyone in sales.

To TeamTY, thank you for encouraging my vision always, for letting me run with scissors, and taking my dreams and finding ways to bring them to fruition bigger and better than I could have dreamed.

Thank you to my Food Network family and to the folks at BSTV for helping me continue to do what I love. Thanks for the opportunity to cook, laugh, and tell stories with my family and friends every week. I'm having a wonderful time! I've learned so much, and I couldn't have a better crew. You know who you are, and I hope you know how much I love you.

Thank you to David Vigliano, for believing I had a fourth cookbook in my brain. To the crew at O'Neil, Hagaman and Co., especially Cheryl Harris and Dana Dennis, thank you for keeping me organized, and special thanks to Rusty Jones for all things legal and all things college football.

Thank you Ben Fink for photographing the food and our family again. I've had the pleasure of watching Beth's children grow up in the pages of my books because of you, and I love you for it. Special thanks to Joe Tully, Brian Eaves, Gabe LaDuke, Gena Sigala, Michelle Warner, Louisa Shafia, Jeanne Kelley, Nicole Ford, and Veronica Carmona for cooking, styling, prepping, shopping, and driving on the Tennessee and California shoots! Russ Harrington, thank you for being my friend (who also happens to be one of the most amazing photographers on the planet!) From album covers to cookbook covers, you are simply the best. Thank you for the lovely cover photograph, and special thanks to Derrick Hood, Matt Harrington, Brent Harrington, Jamie Bayer, and Amanda Frederickson for assisting, styling, and cooking! Thank you Robby Klein and your crew for the beautiful photo you took of Beth and me for the dedication page! Thanks to Ellen Summers for prop styling on the Nashville shoots, and thank you to Earl Cox, Mary Beth Felts, and Claudia Fowler for hair, makeup, and wardrobe on both shoots in Nashville. Callie Blackburn, thank you for organizing and corralling everyone for the shoots, and special thanks to Jarrah Paschall for all you do to keep the house for *Trisha's Kitchen* beautiful! Thank you to Tommy Colorigh for adding just the right amount of retouch love to make us pretty but keep us real! You are so talented.

Michelle Warner, an extra thank you for your friendship. I would not have had the courage to start this book without your constant encouragement and support. You were the friend who told me I had a good book in the making, and you helped me fill in the gaps by talking through new recipes, and helping me develop what we needed along the way. Thank you for helping me while navigating a pandemic, another job, and raising a small human. You are superwoman and everybody knows it!

To the friends and family who contributed recipes and stories to this book, especially Helen Carter, Janet Regard, Janine Terry, Tina Tyler, Tracy Paulk Griffin, Leeann Culbreath, Marcia Pennington, Kathy Rossi, and Mary Berry. Thank you for sharing your family recipes with us. To our families, John, Ashley, Kyle, and Bret; and Garth, Taylor, August, and Allie. Thanks for letting us tell stories about you, and being the best testers the Yearwood sisters could ask for. We love you so very much!

Beth, what it really comes down to is family. None of this happens without you. Thank you for being my collaborator, my cheerleader, my counsel, my sister, my friend. I love you.

Our mom, Gwendolyn's cake sketches, 1960's

Index

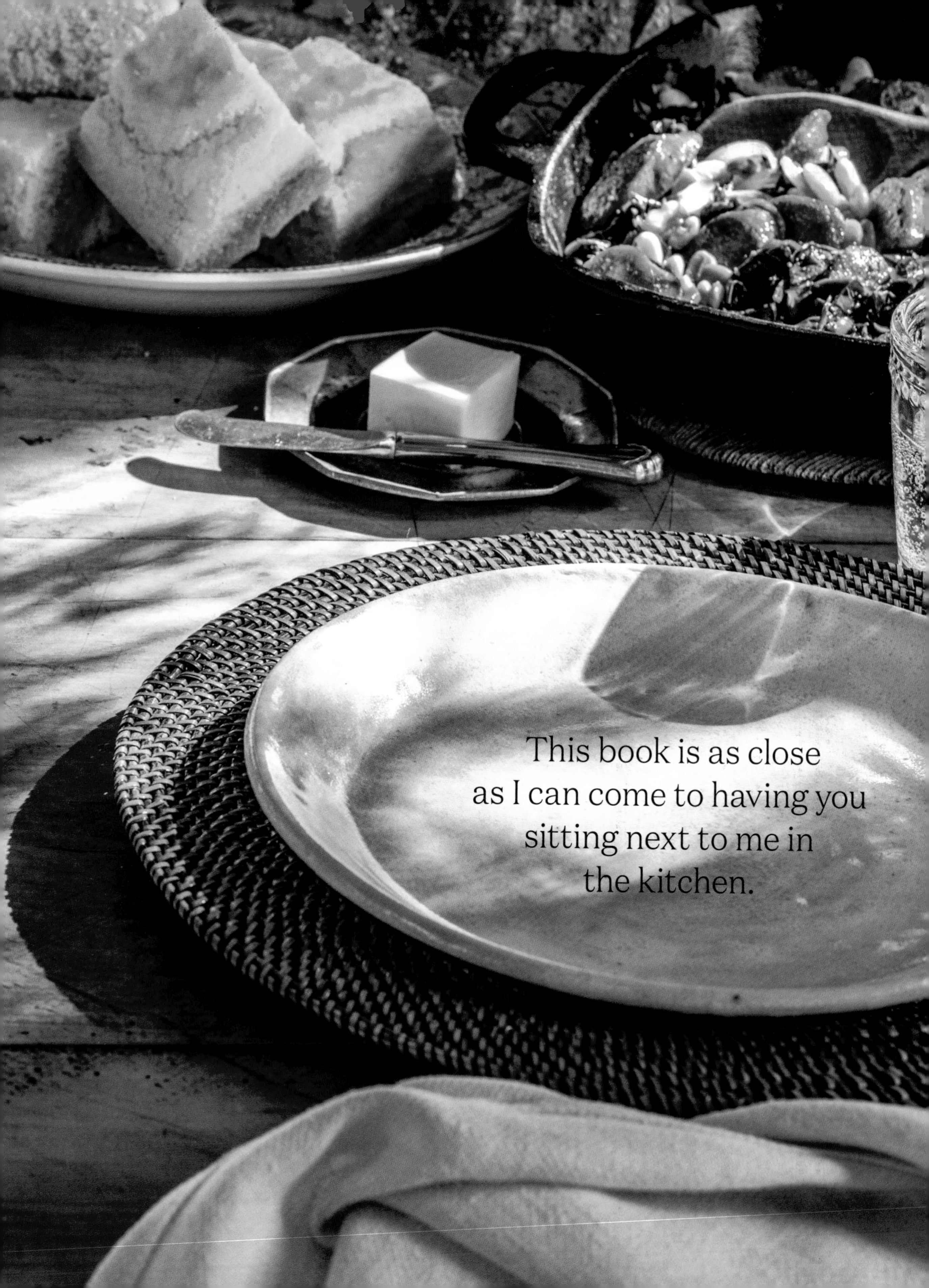

This book is as close
as I can come to having you
sitting next to me in
the kitchen.